I DOUBLE DARE YOU

THE ULTIMATE GUIDE TO CREATING DUPLICATION IN YOUR NETWORK MARKETING BUSINESS.

DEDICATION

To Svetlana, thank you for continuing to be my number one
fan and biggest supporter, I love you.

CONTENTS

Acknowledgements   7

INTRODUCTION

1   I Double Dare You   11

2   Understanding The Numbers   21

PART ONE – I DOUBLE DARE YOU TO BELIEVE IT

3   The Infinity Cycle Of Success   29

4   The Bridge Of Belief   37

5   Increasing Distributor Retention   51

PART TWO – I DOUBLE DARE YOU TO BUILD IT

6   The Robbo Rule   63

7   Exclusive Zoom Event   71

8   Your Social Media Launch   81

9   Duplicatable Systems   89

10 3 Way Messenger Chats   101

PART THREE – I DOUBLE DARE YOU TO BOOST IT

11 Creating Group Momentum   109

12 Tracking Your Numbers   121

13 Events To Skyrocket Your Business   131

14 Blitz's And Challenges   141

15 I Double Dare You To Do It   149

ACKNOWLEDGEMENTS

To all my friends, fans and followers. You make doing what I do an absolute pleasure. This book has taken me 12 months to write. There have been many moments of wanting to give up, but your constant messages and comments of support have really pushed me to become the best version of myself.

As a result, I want you to know, that without that engagement, I wouldn't be where I am today.

This book has been created to help you build a business you are proud of, but most importantly, leave a legacy where people talk about you when you leave the room or your time comes to an end.

To my Mum, Julie, without your constant guidance and mentorship, as well as never ending help and support I would be useless. You make me want to be a better human each and every single day. If I can help others, half as much as you have helped me, the world will be a better place.

To my Dad, Simon, thank you for continuing to tell me how incredible Network Marketing is. Your unwavering belief in this wonderful profession allowed me to see the bigger picture, believe I could do it, and therefore help many around the world realise their full potential.

To Svetlana, none of this would be possible without you. I know when we sat down to edit the book we thought it would never end, but there is no one I would rather go through this process with than you.

INTRODUCTION

CHAPTER 1
I DOUBLE DARE YOU

It's April 2010 and the day had come when I decided to join the Network Marketing profession. After saying no for four years the day had finally arrived, my life wouldn't be the same again. I was so excited.

Fortunately, my Dad was my upline. After joining, I went into his office, and told him the good news, he was happy, and went on to give me my first assignment.

"Frazer, I want you to get a piece of paper and a pen."

I had heard him say this so many times over the years.

"Write down the numbers from 1 to 200 on the left hand side. In the middle, I want you to write down the names of the people you know, not who you think will join, but people you know. Then lastly, on the right hand side, give them a score out of 10, with 10 being super influential, 1 being not very super influential."

It sounded so simple, I felt unstoppable at the time. Joining the business meant I had taken my first step towards greatness.

I went upstairs to my bedroom, sat at my desk, and started to write down all the names of people I knew.

As I began to write the list, a sense of excitement passed through my body. However, I was also filled with nerves knowing I would have to contact these people.

Some of the names had a huge circle of friends. Their influence was much greater than mine. They had so many more contacts than I could ever dream of.

Being 22 years old at the time, I didn't know so many people. I was told to aim for 200. The size of my first list was 137 names.

I returned to my Dad's office with, my now filled, pieces of paper. I had a big smile on my face, thinking, "This is it. These 137 people are going to be responsible for building the world's biggest and best Network Marketing empire the world has ever seen."

My Dad looked at the list, smiled and looked back at me. It was an emotional moment, my Dad had been waiting for the day he would build a business with his son. It was also a proud moment for me.

But it didn't last long.

As he started to read the list, I could see his face turn from super excitement to one of concern.

"Frazer, we have a problem."

I replied somewhat confused, "What? What's happened, Dad?"

At this stage I am thinking I've only just started my Network Marketing career and already have an issue. There is a problem.

He looked up at me and said, "You know you've got 137 names here."

I said, "Yeah, of course. I wrote them."

He laughed, "Well you know as a network marketer, what do you think I do whenever you introduce me to a friend of yours?"

"Well, you probably speak to them," I replied having suddenly realised something, "You've spoken to people on my list already haven't you?"

He started to count the people on the list.

I asked him , "How many Dad? Like 10, 20?"

He started to laugh, "No, no. More than that."

I was now concerned, "What? 40, 50?"

"No, a lot more." He replied.

A short moment of silence later he looked up at me and said "Ok, I've just added it up. It's 102 people."

I was shocked.

The list of 137 people I thought would be responsible for creating the world's greatest Network Marketing empire is now going to be 35 people. I thought that was it. My journey, my

Network Marketing career was over before I've even began.

My Dad stood up, walked to me from around his desk, put his hands on my shoulders and said something that I have now shared with people all over the world.

The money is not in the list, the money is in the skills that you create from the list.

That was the first big lesson I learned.

He continued by saying that your business will really begin when you've finished your list. "There are more people in this world that you do not know than you do know. So let's get contacting your list, and go from there."

It's a game of skillset and mindset.

My skillset was zero, and my mindset had taken a huge beating, but I needed to get to work. I was hungry for a change in my life, and if you're reading this right now I guess you are hungry for change in your life too.

My Dad then gave me my next assignment.

"Frazer, we've got some free time tonight. Why don't you invite four of your mates who live locally around to the house?"

The panic started to set in, "What do I do?"

He said, "Just do whatever feels natural. Say whatever you would to get your friends to the house."

Although that was nothing new to me, I felt uncomfortable.

My Dad asked "How do you usually speak to your mates? Call or Text?"

I said, "we all chat with text."

He then made things super simple and said just send them this message:

"Hey mate, what are you doing at eight o'clock tonight?"

Is that really it, I started to think as I looked at my Dad.

I opened up my phone, wrote the message out, and sent it, my Dad wouldn't let me leave his office until I had sent the four messages.

Within minutes I received a message from one of my mates saying, "Oh, well the football's on."

I replied, "Great. Do you fancy watching it at mine? The rest of the lads are coming here, and at the end of the game I've got something really exciting I want to share with you."

I had my first appointment arranged and confirmed, I couldn't believe it, but my Dad seemed so calm, he laughed and said "Why wouldn't he want to come see you? He's your friend."

He was right, I was just trying to over complicate it by trying to learn how to be perfect.

Focus on progression, as perfection is not possible.

A few moments passed, and friend number two confirmed. Two out of two.

Friend number three confirmed. Three out of three.

Friend number four confirmed. Four out of four. I was loving this. I had a 100% record.

Eight o'clock arrived, and my four mates were now at the house. The football is on and everything is great. Two hours later one of the lads asked, "So what's this thing you wanted to talk to us about?"

Panic set in, I thought my Dad would be coming in to do the presentation, he was the master, I was a disaster. I left the room to find my Dad, but he was nowhere to be seen. He had gone out!

I had no choice! I had to do the presentation, so I ended up giving the world's worst presentation, it was terrible.

There were no slides, no information about how things work, I just shared what I was excited about and why I decided to get involved as well as my reasons why I wanted my friends to get involved too.

If you knew me before I started Network Marketing, I was the quietest person in the room. I was really shy, super introverted, didn't like being around a group of people, and I absolutely hated being the focus of attention.

But I was so enthusiastic. I truly believed this business could change my life, and I felt I was doing a disservice to my friends if I was to keep it a secret.

One of my best friends said "I have never seen you so excited, I'm in, let's do this."

There was a party happening inside of me, I couldn't believe I was about to get my first sign up.

Then my other three friends said they were in too.

It was magical, I couldn't believe it. Was I now the most un-stoppable network marketer on the planet?

My friends joined that night, I got my first rank advancement, then my Dad returned home. I couldn't wait to tell him the news, he was thrilled, he told all his other team the story, I was so happy.

My Dad then showed me something extremely powerful.

He walked over to his desk, got a pack of playing cards from the top drawer, and started to shuffle them.

"Frazer, you have just turned over 4 Aces. Chances are, the next few messages you send out won't go so well."

I was about to learn my next lesson.

I now had to contact the other 133 people on my list. The only rule was that I had to go through five people at a time and report to my Dad with an update.

Easy, I had a 100% record, I was unstoppable.

I contacted the next five, they all rejected me, that hurt. My 100% record had ended and it will never return. I felt my confi-dence had been knocked. Why wouldn't someone want to join this business or use this product?

"You have just turned over 5 of the other cards, all the Aces are gone from this pack" my Dad reiterated to me.

He had set the expectations that I was going to fail with the rest of my list, he had created a win-win situation.

I wanted to prove him wrong, but if I didn't get anyone else join he would have shown me that I need to listen to him and be coachable.

I contacted the next five, they all rejected me again, then I spoke to my Dad, we discussed, it hurt a little less.

Next five, same thing, all rejected, updated my Dad, we discussed, I noticed it didn't hurt so much.

I repeated the process with all 137 people from my list, the first four people joined, the other 133 said no. Ouch!

My Dad reminded me that this business requires a strong skillset as well as an unbreakable mindset.

My list had ended, but I knew my business was now about to begin.

I then made a mistake.

I believed my four friends would be just like me, have the hunger and desire like me, and I could just help them do the same as I did and things would multiply.

So here's the problem.

My friends were people I spent a lot of time with, and although that's not really a problem, the problem was, that I did everything with these friends and the majority of the time was spent in the pub watching the football.

Whenever we did our brainstorming meetings, we were in the pub.

Whenever we did our accountability meetings, we were in the pub.

Whenever the company did a training and we were on it, we were in the pub.

Whenever we had a bad week, we went to the pub.

Whenever we wanted to celebrate, we were in the pub.

After about two weeks, my team of four had turned into ten. However the other six people who were in the business were people who were just supporting their sons.

I realised that the team had pretty much done nothing, and I needed to figure out a way how to create duplication, because my Dad goes traveling all over the world and his business continued to grow.

If I was to go on a holiday for a month, my business would die because my team would think, "Where's Frazer? Where's our leader?"

My team were dependent on me, yet when they joined they signed the form stating they were independent distributors.

One night coming home from the pub (again), we drove past the McDonald's, we stopped and walked in. I ordered the 20 chicken nuggets and the guy I gave the order to was a spotty teenager who looked like he was half asleep.

He looked like he'd just finished smoking a spliff. He did not look capable of taking an order.

He turns his back, gets the fries, drink, chicken nuggets, and returns. He grabs the sauces, puts it all on the tray and nailed it. It was perfect.

Now, my initial reaction was judging this guy. I shouldn't judge people. But my second reaction, which was stronger was these guys have got a system. These guys have got a process where they know what they have to do in order to succeed. That is to create a good customer experience so they keeping coming back, as well as tell their friends to check it out.

From that moment, I worked on the master plan to get people started and duplicate the process.

This book reveals that exact plan, which has been tweaked over the years, to give you the absolute best shot at creating massive duplication in your business.

If you want my masterplan on recruiting people using social media be sure to check out my first book, I Dare You, using this link; frazerbrookes.com/book

I cannot wait to share with you my three step process on how you can get the unshakeable **belief**, how you can **build** your business like crazy with a duplicable system, and how you can **boost** that in order to create duplication throughout your organisation so you can truly live the life on your terms.

CHAPTER 2
UNDERSTANDING THE NUMBERS

It used to frustrate me like crazy when I would recruit a bunch of people, they would be excited, then they would do absolutely nothing and quit.

I actually preferred getting a "no", than getting someone join and then quit!

No one would show the same ambition or hunger as myself. No one would share the same drive.

It seemed like I was fighting a losing battle. I'd recruit 10, 20, 30 people and have no sort of system, no process.

The reality is that there will be more people who will do nothing, than do something.

Recently, one of my friends, Eric Worre, the founder of Network Marketing Pro, shared with me some statistics that completely shocked me.

- 70% of people who join the Network Marketing profession will recruit zero people into their business.

- 20% will recruit in between 1–2 people into their business.
- 5% will recruit between 3–5 people in their business.
- 3% will recruit in between 6–9 people into their business.
- Only 2% will recruit 10 people or more into their business.
- The average person in the 2% recruits 27 people.

This proves that 70% will do absolutely nothing in terms of recruiting.

One of the reasons why people get frustrated is because so many people are sharing the message of:

"All you need to do is get three, who get three, who get three."

People fall for this and it sets the wrong expectations which is harming our wonderful profession. Please stop it.

The stats above show that only 10% of people will ever get three or more recruits in their career so the three, who get three, who get three is a complete myth.

I was always trying to duplicate people, when really I needed a duplicatable system to identify who the runners were, help them identify their runners, and so on.

Based on the numbers above if you were to recruit 100 people personally in your career you could expect the following:

- 70 do absolutely nothing
- 20 recruit 1 or 2, so approximately 30 distributors join your team
- 5 recruit 3 to 5, so approximately 20 distributors join your team

- 3 recruit 6 to 9, so approximately 22 distributors join your team
- 2 recruit 27, so approximately 54 distributors join your team.

Which means 126 distributors join your team on your second level coming from your front line, so if you keep repeating this process each level grows by 20-30%, not 300% like the message most network marketers are putting out.

There is a common question that a lot of network marketers ask me, and that is:

"Should I focus on building width, or depth."

In simple terms, should I focus on recruiting or developing my team so they duplicate.

There is a saying that "width is for show, and depth is for dough". Broken down this means when you recruit a lot you get the attention for being a top producer, but it's the duplication that creates the long term income.

I like to use the golf analogy to explain this better.

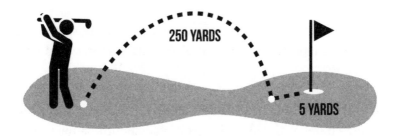

250 YARDS

5 YARDS

You stand on the first tee, your ball is teed up, you get your golf driver out of the bag, you swing the club, and whack, the ball goes 250 yards. You are then on the green, 5 yards from the hole, it takes you 2 shots to get it in the hole.

One shot to get 250 yards, two shots to get 5 yards.

It doesn't matter how far you can hit the ball from the tee, it only matters how many putts it takes to get the ball into the hole.

Driving is for show, putting is for dough.

I personally believe recruiting in "classes" is the best approach.

A short 30 day blast with a big focus on recruiting, followed by another 30 day blast where developing those new recruits is the focus as well as recruiting the next class.

My first book will help you with the recruiting, this book will help you with the duplicatable system and process.

Since being in the industry as a generic coach, speaker and trainer since the beginning of 2017 I have spent a lot of time analysing the top income earners to see what way is best, and a combination is best.

Just work the numbers, keep track of your own business too, and understand that most people, no matter what, will disappoint you.

Your bare minimum should be 27 personal recruits. That's the average number the top 2% recruit, that should be the standard. Your team will also do what they see you doing, do you want them to be in the 2% or the 70%?

Obviously, if you recruit more people you will be more likely to find the runners. However if you don't have a system to identify them, you could get very frustrated, very quickly.

I Double Dare You to build a minimum of 5 legs wide, with 5 leaders in each leg. This will help you build stability, which will turn into security and freedom.

Perhaps it'll take you a few years, maybe ten or more, but it'll be worth it.

Build the width to begin with, then you can work on the depth. It's the depth that's going to create the long-term income for you.

I believe one of the best systems you have to create inside of your Network Marketing business is one to be able to identify the next success story.

You need to be able to identify the person who is going to take the necessary action, as well as who you need to be pouring into. The reality is, you won't be able to work with everyone who joins your team, and most people will try to drain your time and energy.

1. Recruit in 30 day blasts to create the classes
2. Help them launch individually
3. Mentor those who are taking action
4. Understand that some just want to be a part of the community
5. Repeat

Your personal production time should be spent recruiting. Your individual team time should be spent mentoring those who are taking action to build the business. The rest of the team time can be spent focused on building your community and making the masses feel part of the team. Don't forget them, they are the biggest part of your team.

Now we understand the numbers and realise that we have to recruit, launch, and mentor in order to build the width and depth. In the next chapter you will uncover how to truly believe in the process.

PART ONE

I DOUBLE DARE YOU TO BELIEVE IT

CHAPTER 3
THE INFINITY CYCLE OF SUCCESS

I used to constantly hear one sentence that leaders would say to their team when they felt stuck, weren't progressing or didn't know what to do next. Chances are you would have heard it too:

"Just take massive action!"

Yes, action is the key. Whenever you study what the top income earners in the profession do, it all comes back to action. Without it, success wouldn't be possible. But you have to understand what needs to happen before the action takes place.

Network Marketing is one of the greatest vehicles for people to change their families future for generations with the power of residual income. Being paid time and time again for the work you did once, like actors or songwriters.

If you just take the time to believe it, build it and boost it with your Network Marketing business, you'll be able to potentially create a residual income stream that can pay you and your family time and time and time again.

Think of the infinity symbol, it's like an aerial view of a Scalextric track. If you start the car anywhere on the track and keep driving, there is no end, unless you fall off the track.

We have to be able to identify the steps that allows you to go round and round the track collecting a commission every time you pass the crossover point.

Now the starting point is belief and vision, without this you will simply not take action.

When you have the belief in yourself, your business, your product, your company, your system, and in the people you work with, then you will start to take action.

Side note. If you believe in all the above and aren't taking action in your business it's either because you just want to be a product user, you just want to attend the events, be a part of the community or you don't believe wholeheartedly in what it is that you're doing.

Step one, believe.

Step two is action. This is the crossover point of the infinity symbol, the key step, without it you will not collect the commission.

Step three is experience. In life, whenever you do something, you gain more experience. Think of when you went on your first date. Maybe you were excited, nervous or both. But the more dates you went on the more experience you got and this led to you gaining more confidence.

Step four is confidence. This is created from competence which comes from the experience you have gained.

When you have gained the confidence, you will get more belief that you can actually do it. So for example, you sit in front of your computer, look down at your list, you see your friends name, Bob, now you have to contact him.

"You've got this!" you say to yourself. Belief, done. You might need to leverage the belief of your upline or support line the first few times.

You message Bob.

"Hey Bob, what are you up to tonight at 8:00 PM?"

Action, done.

He replies saying, "Not much, what about you?"

"Not much either, do you fancy grabbing a drink at the local pub?"

Bob replies, "Yeah, sure."

Experience, done. Confidence to do it again, done.

Now it's time for you to meet up with Bob. You get a bit nervous because you want to bring up the business or product with him, but you start thinking about being rejected.

You remember that it all starts with believing in what you are doing. You are doing your friend a disservice by not bringing this up with him. Maybe they are desperate for something to help their pain, financially, mentally or physically.

Belief, done.

You say, "Hey, by the way, glad we got the chance to meet up because I've just gotten started with something and I think you'd be awesome at it. Do you fancy hearing more?"

Action, done.

Here is the important part. Whatever the reaction and response you get back is all adding to your experience, which leads to confidence because you are getting better.

You must detach yourself from their response, and be obsessed about your actions.

Some people say, "marry the process, and divorce the result."

Many will get a negative reaction or response from their contacts, and let it affect their confidence and therefore their belief, so their action is reduced, in most cases, to nothing.

This is why it is so important, as an upline, to ensure your new team member contacts you after every person they speak to about the business or product.

You are going to have to give your belief, experience and confidence to your new team member so that they can leverage it to take the necessary action.

The more someone takes action through the negative responses the stronger they will become.

The strongest, most powerful network marketers are the ones who have worked through the pain, rejection, isolation and embarrassment the most.

Getting rejections and objections is only going to make you stronger.

It's like being a gladiator in the colosseum. Your sword is your invitation, and your shield is your objection handling. Every time you take action and give out an invitation your skills improve. Every time you deal with rejection or an objection, your shield gets bigger.

With time, you will get more acceptance from your invitations, and the negativity doesn't make a mark on you.

It will always hurt more in the beginning.

Hearing, "it sounds like one of those pyramid things" is only going to weed out the weak, or make the right ones stronger.

Just remember as the responsible upline, mentor or support partner, your job is to guide them through the questions, responses and objections that are going to come up.

Let's move on to the other side of the infinity symbol.

Step five is speed. When you take a large amount of action you create speed. Think of when you are in a plane about to take off, there is a sudden acceleration before you take off. Success loves speed and when a large amount of action is condensed into a short space of time this creates momentum.

Step six is momentum. This is the fundamental step to reach in this process to turbo boost your Network Marketing business. Not only will results start coming in faster than ever before, but the energy within the organisation goes through the roof. With this crazy wave of momentum comes the last step.

Step seven is excitement. When your team is waking up excited to get to work, and going to bed excited for the next day, that's when the magic starts to happen. The events are better, the trainings are incredible, everyone is loving on each other, and of course, people are taking more action.

Which completes the cycle.

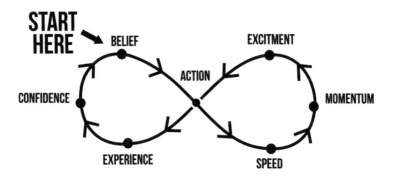

The belief has helped us take action, which has given us the experience necessary to create the confidence to therefore believe in ourselves more. This means we take more action, which then helps us to build more speed, leading to momentum, generating a large amount of excitement and causing everyone to take action again, therefore gaining more experience faster and the process continues.

Removing the belief, the action will not be taken. Without the action, we don't create the necessary experience to move forward. You have to believe in yourself. If you don't, you won't win.

This whole process reminds me of when I was growing up, in my teens.

I really wanted to date a particular girl. I debated it with myself for about two weeks, I had a lack of belief. Eventually I decided to ask her out and she said, "yes".

We went on a first date. It was great.

A few more dates went by, and now I was getting a bit of peer pressure from my friends of saying, "Hey, you've gone on four or five dates now. When are you going to take her back to your house for a 'coffee'?"

I remember having no belief. I was excited by the idea. I wanted to do it, but I didn't believe in myself. I didn't believe in what I had to do. I didn't believe in the reaction. I didn't believe in the circumstances. I didn't believe in what she would say.

But I made that leap of faith and I believed in myself to ask her back to my place. We took certain action, which therefore gave me more experience and that more experience, made me confident to believe in my own ability and my skills to want to do the action again.

When I was doing that action again, I started to notice I was generating more speed, which led to a little bit of momentum and then I got excited and took action. So it doesn't just work in the Network Marketing space. It works in all areas of life.

Let's look at it in the fitness space. You don't believe in yourself, what if you'll be the most overweight person there? What if you are lifting the lightest weights? This makes you feel that you are not confident enough in front of other people who are clearly bigger and better at this game than you are.

But you pluck up enough courage to believe in yourself that

you can go and you take action, you go to the gym. When you come out, you get an experience of what it's like for the first time and it gives you more confidence to go back. So you believe in yourself that you can actually do it.

By taking more action generates more speed in your regime. You get into momentum in your nutrition plan, your diet plan, your exercise plan, which then gets you excited because you start to see your results, which then makes you want to take more action. You eliminate the bad foods. You bring in the good foods, you go to the gym more, you walk more, you run more, you move more, you stretch more, you meditate more, and it's a cycle again.

It's a health cycle, Network Marketing success cycle; relationship cycle. It works with everything. Everything starts in believing in yourself.

As the upline, if you can give some of your belief into your new team member, you will dramatically increase the chances of them taking the necessary activity. But how? In this next chapter I will introduce you to the "Bridge Of Belief".

CHAPTER 4
THE BRIDGE OF BELIEF

I want to introduce you to a concept of mine to really help you appreciate and understand that belief is a set of actions and not just thoughts.

There's a lot of people out there who say, "I believe I'm going to succeed. I've got all the belief. I love my company, I love my product." But they don't actually take action. And as I said in the previous chapter, the whole concept of taking action stems from belief.

Imagine, there are two lands: Loser Land and Success Land.

Now as you can see from the image, Loser Land is on the left and Success Land is on the right and in between both of these lands is a treacherous river that contains sharks, piranhas, crocodiles, all of the dangerous creatures. It's probably somewhere in Australia!

Everyone starts on Loser Land. Why? I know you're not a loser. But when you got started on your Network Marketing journey you had no customers, no distributors, and no Network Marketing experience.

In almost all sports, if you have zero, it means that you have not got started, or you will have lost the game, right? So when you start Network Marketing, you have zero customers, you have zero distributors, you have zero Network Marketing experience.

Guess what? I started with a bunch of zeros.

Eric Worre had the same. Jim Rohn too.

Here's the thing, all of your friends, your family, your colleagues, they are also on Loser Land. However, over on Success Land, across the water is your upline, your mentor, the leaders in your company.

They keep shouting over to you, "Frazer, just jump. I did. Make the leap of faith. Just have the belief in me, and the system."

But as much as you love the look of life over on Success Land, all that you're thinking about is, what if I fall? What if I don't make it? What happens if I don't succeed?

I'm going to die. The sharks are going to get me. The piranhas are going to eat me up. One snap from those crocodiles and it's over for me.

Your friends, family and everyone else you know are saying, "No, don't do it. Stay here. It's more comfortable here. You don't want to lose. You don't want to risk. What happens if you become a failure?"

You have to create your own Bridge Of Belief.

Now, if you followed me for some time, you'll know that I use two names a lot. Bob and Mary, well Bob is actually an acronym, Bridge Of Belief. So if you've ever wondered now you know. Belief is simply that important.

There are seven steps to building your own Bridge Of Belief, to go from Loser Land, to Success Land.

Step one is you have to be a product of the product or service.

If you don't, start to use it every single day. When you believe in something so much, you do whatever it takes to take action on it. Think about brushing your teeth. You believe that brushing them daily is going to keep your teeth clean and breath fresh. If you were to brush your teeth on Monday and not bother for the rest of the week, you would have a problem, and probably lose some friends!

Once you have taken the first step across the bridge, you're going to face the first problem. Your friends, family and acquaintances will start to shout, "Frazer, stay here. Stay here."

Your upline however will be shouting, "No, Frazer, come here.

Come here."

You are only one step across the bridge. Your friends and family on Loser Land are closer to you. They're louder in your head. They're making more noise. So you will have a tendency to listen to the people who are on Loser Land and ignore the noise that you can hear from your mentor.

People will try to limit your success in order to keep their power.

Most people will go back to Loser Land and give up because of people who think they know what's best for them.

The right people will ignore the noise, focus on where they want to go, and make it happen.

Step two is to contact your upline every day. Now, what happens if you don't have an upline? You should go to your most active upline. If you don't have an active upline, then partner with a side line or a down line to hold each other accountable.

If you still don't have someone to partner with, then you have to become that partner to others who you wish you had.

A lot of belief and taking action is having accountability. Over the years I have seen many cases of people who have succeeded just by checking in with their uplines on a consistent basis.

You're two steps across the bridge. You use a product or service every single day, and you contact your upline, side line or down line every single day. But still, you are closer to Loser Land. So when the crowds start shouting, "Frazer stay here." And your upline, mentor, leader says, "No, Frazer, come here."

The Loser Land voices and noise is still louder in your head.

Step three is to attend some sort of event every single month. Whether it's online or offline, make sure you are there, non-negotiable. You have to make sure you are staying plugged into the system.

Imagine this. There's a desk fan on your desk right now and it's plugged in. The fan is going round and round. Then you unplugged the desk fan.

Will the fan stop? Not immediately. No, it slows down and slows down and then eventually it stops.

The process of attending an online or offline event every month is you ensuring that stay plugged in so that the desk fan does not stop. If it was to stop that's the moment you have lost belief, and don't take action.

You're now three steps across the Bridge Of Belief. The people on Loser Land they continue to shout, "Frazer, stay here." Over on Success Land they're shouting, "Frazer come here."

You start to notice that the voice of "come here" in your head is becoming louder and louder. But still, the noises from Loser Land, are louder.

Maybe you start thinking you are not worthy. Perhaps you start doubting your abilities. What if my friends won't like me anymore?

The fear of failure is there to push you to succeed rather than to pull you back to failure.

As always, the right people will continue across the Bridge Of Belief.

Step four is get a new personal customer every single month. Right now you might be seeing this as a struggle, but if you complete steps one, two and three, this will become much more simple.

If you are not sharing your product experience with others, on social media or in person then you don't truly believe in what you have to offer. Network Marketing companies rely on you to tell the world based on your good experience.

Go check out my first book 'I Dare You' for more tips on using social media to build your Network Marketing business.

The cool thing is you are now in the middle of the bridge, so when the noise comes in, when the people over on Loser Land scream out, "Frazer stay here." And Success Land, "Frazer come here". You have a decision to make, as the noise is equal in your head.

You might feel confused, you might feel overwhelmed. So you look back to Loser Land and you look at your friends, family and acquaintance doing the exact same thing, week in, week out. You then turn around and you look to Success Land to see your upline driving the nice cars, living debt free, traveling around the world, going on all the incentive trips making an impact and you make a decision.

You don't go back. You decide to walk straight to where you need to go.

Step five is you get a new distributor every single month.

Perhaps you're thinking, "Oh yeah, but a new personal customer, and a new personal distributor every single month. That's really difficult."

Here's what I know.

If you believe in what you are doing wholeheartedly, 100% you will tell the world about what it is you're doing. If you believe Shawshank Redemption is the best movie, you will tell everyone about it. If you believe Don Louigi's Italian restaurant does the best spaghetti carbonara, you will tell everyone about it. If you believe that your wife or husband, is the best partner ever, you will tell everyone about it, right? You believe in it, 100%. Period.

This creates the conviction necessary for people to believe in you enough to buy. But there will still be those who will resist just for the sake of resisting.

If you don't believe 100% that's why you're not getting the results. Because belief creates the activity. Big belief, big activity. No belief, no activity.

No one has ever succeeded without having 100% belief in what they're doing.

Usain Bolt did not break the 100 meter sprint world record by not believing that he could do it.

You're five steps across the Bridge Of Belief. You look back to Loser Land. They're shouting, "Stay here Frazer. Stay here." It's like a whisper to you. Success Land is deafeningly loud and now you are so focused on getting there.

Step six is to attend some sort of company convention. Whether it's a small regional, decent sized national, or even a big international event. It doesn't matter if it's your first one or your 100th one. You have to attend one every single year. It's fundamental.

It's kind of crazy now. You can't even see the people on Loser Land and you start to look at Success Land. You begin to look at it so intently and so directly that you know that is where you need to be. You've never felt so focussed in your entire life.

You're about to take the final step of the Bridge Of Belief.

Step seven is to hear the CEO, owner, or founder(s) speak. When they speak the words are heard differently. There is no one who has a bigger vision than them from a company perspective. They created it, or have had a significant part to play. They have the belief in what they are doing and they have to pass that belief and vision to you.

When you hear from the people who are captaining the team, driving the ship, or flying the plane you buy into their mission. You want to be a part of it, and you want to share the message with the rest of the world.

This is the final step to believing. If you go all in, you're going to get paid for generations.

Congratulations. You are now on Success Land. It's fun, warm and sunny, everyone is happy and positive. You find a palm tree, you get a nice cold beverage and sit in the shade to watch the world go by.

You watch the sunrise, the sunset, you swim with turtles, go on a jet ski, perhaps you read a book whilst in a hammock.

But you are about to face your next problem.

Such a huge percentage of people in Network Marketing fall into this trap.

Just like your upline did to you in the beginning. You go and shout over to Loser Land, "Come on, just jump. I did, make the leap of faith. Just have the belief in me, have the belief in the system."

Be careful, don't become a cheerleader, be a real leader.

You have to get up off your backside, appreciate that Success Land is going to be there waiting for you, and now you have to walk back over your own Bridge Of Belief. Pick up one of your friends from Loser Land and then help them create their own Bridge Of Belief by showing them the steps.

So you get one of your 'Loser Land' friends, Jane. Remember, Jane is not a loser, she just lives on 'Loser Land', for now, and you walk her through the steps.

Step one be a product of the product.

Jane replies "I don't like the way it smells. I don't like the taste. I don't like how it feels on my face. I prefer to shop on Amazon. I prefer the coffee that I drink in Starbucks. I prefer this and that".

Do you try to drag people across? Do you try to put a funnel in their mouth and pour the potions or drink down their throat? No, you simply push them off the bridge.

Now in this case, you might think you're killing them. You're throwing them into the sharks. No, you are just basically saying that you are not going to waste your time with those people.

You have to work with the action takers and forget the action fakers.

You need to run with the runners. You need to put your belief into other people who put their belief in the actions you're sharing with them. This is the fundamental step in belief. This is the fundamental step in duplication, and then hence why I spend a lot of time talking about it in this book.

Back to Loser Land you go. You pick up another friend. Step one, product of the product. "Ooh, I really like this product. It's fantastic. Thank you for introducing me".

Second step, contact me every single day. They say, "yeah, great, I'll do that".

But remember, meanwhile they're having their own fight with Loser Land.

This is why you need to walk them through every step of the way. Imagine if you are next to them whispering into their ear "come with me, I will take you to Success Land".

If you stay on Success Land and shout over to them, you limit your chances of getting people over, and therefore gaining duplication.

Your friends however will start to say, "why are you speaking to that guy? We've known you all your life. You've only known him for three days and you're listening to him more than you're listening to us."

Your new team mate, might start thinking, "yeah, you're right. Why am I listening to this complete stranger? He only seems to tell me what's best for him."

You're going to have to appreciate that some will return to Loser Land because they are not ready yet. Most will give up and fail.

So you just have to keep going back to Loser Land, recruit someone into your team and walk them over their own Bridge Of Belief.

There will be issues at different stages.

"I'm not going to come to the events. All my friends say that it's a cult and that they're trying to brainwash me."

The simple answer to that is, "Hey, question, do you ever wash your body because it gets dirty? So why shouldn't you wash your brain when it gets dirty full of negativity?"

It might take you recruiting five to twenty people to get one person to make it all the way to Success Land. You will have kicked a lot of people off the bridge.

They will be in the team Facebook group. They can get the generic information that's shared. Updates, training calls, information on team events and so on. But you shouldn't be wasting your time trying to push people across the bridge.

Finally, you get someone with you over to Success Land. Claire made it.

You will now face another problem.

You either both sit underneath the palm tree and drink pina coladas together while the sunrises and sunsets. Isn't that fun.

Or you say, "Go on Claire. What I want you to do is to go back over to Loser Land, get a Loser Land friend and bring them back to Success Land. I'll cheer you on. I'm here if you need".

No, you need to do it with them again.

You both walk back over to Loser Land. You get a friend, you help Claire get a friend and you show her with your actions that you believe in what they're doing. You believe in them and you help Claire kick people off the bridge.

You help her find people to go to the first step, second, third, fourth, and so on until she knows how to get people onto Success Land.

Now you have duplication based on belief. Your job as the leader is to:

1. Walk across your own Bridge Of Belief
2. Walk back to Loser Land to recruit someone
3. Show them the steps to walk across their own Bridge Of Belief
4. Kick those off the bridge if they aren't following the process, and into the Facebook group where they get the mass support
5. Help the right people walk back to Loser Land from Success Land to repeat the process.

As I covered in the previous chapter, vision and belief is what creates the activity, which is now going to create experience in your team. Turning into team confidence, team belief, team action, team speed, team momentum, team excitement and therefore more action, which is the key.

In the next chapter, I want to talk to you about how do you increase the retention so that you reduce the number of people who are actually quitting the business once joining.

CHAPTER 5
INCREASING DISTRIBUTOR RETENTION

As I travel around the world, there are four big problems that people seem to face when they build a Network Marketing business:

1. Lead Generation
2. Recruiting
3. Duplication
4. Retention

My first book, I Dare You, was all about the first two points, and this book mainly covers the third point, duplication. So I wanted to share some of the methods that I've been able to help people implement when it comes to retention.

I think it's crucial that you get things in place so that you can retain as many of the people who join the organisation as possible. As I shared earlier in Chapter two, not everyone's going to do something, but you don't want to lose those people.

You want to create an environment that people don't want to leave.

More often than not, the issue is not with the seed, but with the soil.

Too many people in Network Marketing are focused on be-coming a better seed and forgetting how important the soil is. The environment and the energy you create is everything.

Imagine if I get the world's best seed and I put it in between two rocks, is it going to grow? No. But if I take the world's worst seed and I put it in the best soil possible, it can turn into a big tall tree which will flourish for many years.

It is also important to remember that the day you plant the seed is not the day you eat the fruit.

You are going to have to understand that it's a game, and lead-ers are seeders.

Leaders plant seeds every single day. They water them, they nurture them and then they are proud of the ones that grow into big tall trees. We have to create a better soil.

There are four stages in order to increase distributor retention, and to get the team locked into the process and community as much as possible.

The first stage is to get people to believe they are in the right place by helping them get emotionally connected to the busi-ness. You have to get really good at becoming a mentor.

I believe mentorship, at the time of writing this book, is actually a dying art. People are trying to shortcut the process by being too broad, too automated, and pressing a button to go live to get their message out to 100 plus people. Instead of spending the time with the right people to actually walk them through the steps.

When someone joins the team, you have no idea if they're going to be a success or not. There is a saying in the business world, "hiring is guessing, firing is knowing".

I believe similar to be true in Network Marketing:

"Recruiting is guessing, working with the right people is knowing!"

The first stage of becoming a mentor is to recruit someone. After that, instead of sending a link, or adding to a group and letting the new rep figure it all out by themselves, you need to get on a call with them and spend 15 to 30 minutes establishing what the reason for joining is.

Some people will say "you need to find your why that makes you cry". I prefer to ask the question, "what hurts you?" then continue to ask "why is that important" to get to their true reason why.

Keep repeating until they can't keep answering the questions, you will then have helped them uncover the true reason as to why they want to do the business.

HERE'S HOW IT WORKS.

"Hey Frazer, what's hurting me right now is I am struggling with finances. I want financial freedom."

You would say, "Why? Why is financial freedom important to you?"

They might say something like, "Oh, it's because it means I'm going to be able to travel the world with my kids."

Again, you would ask "Why do you want to do that?"

"Well, because then I will be able to create great memories with my kids".

You would reply with, "Why is that important to you?"

There might be a pause, then your new team member comes back with, "Well, I know my Mum and Dad said when they were on their deathbed that they wish they'd travelled more as a family."

BINGO!

Your goal is to solve the problem your new team member has in their life right now so that you can share the next steps for them to make it happen. This enables them to get emotionally connected to the business and mission.

Knowing this also allows you to create a sentence that you will say back to them when they have those moments of doubt, where they come close to quitting.

"Hey Bob, is (enter their WHY here), still important to you?"

In our example above this would be:

"Hey Bob, is travelling the world with your kids still important to you?"

That's it, you are telling them they will be quitting on what's really important to them, more time with their kids, world travel, becoming debt free, and so on.

If you don't know their why you won't be able to say the above sentence to them.

I always remember as a kid, I used to sometimes stay at my grandparent's house on a Friday night. At a certain time, my granddad would go to the fish and chip shop, buy a couple of fish for us all and then two big bags of chips. He'd come home and my grandmother would shout, "Wash hands."

Now wash hands was a sign that dinner is ready and we had to go and wash our hands with soap before we could obviously pick at the food.

I remember hitting a certain age, I was probably six or seven, and saying to my grandmother, "Why? Why do I have to wash my hands?"

She said, "Because they're dirty."

"Why? Why do I have to wash my hands of the dirt?" I replied.

She answered, "Because you have to get rid of the bad bacteria."

I said, "But why?"

"Because if you touch the food, you and the rest of the people touching the food will get poorly." She said whilst hurrying me to the bathroom.

"And why does that matter?" I asked.

She stopped me, got down to my level, and said "Well, if you're not feeling great, you won't be able to go to school. You won't be able to play with your friends."

Washing my hands would prevent me spending time with my friends. That's the importance of using the simple question of why, to get deeper.

More often than not people will have a breakdown, before they have a breakthrough, and you helping them connect emotionally to the business will lock them in faster than anything else.

The second stage is for you to create a good feeling.

Once they believe they are actually in the right place after joining, you now need to create a good feeling that they don't necessarily get anywhere else.

I have a very simple acronym, called FAR. In order for you to go FAR:

- you need to get a good **feeling**
- which helps you take **action**,
- which then helps you get the **results**.

The best way of getting this important good feeling is by attending an event.

When you're on the first call, helping your new team member connect to their why, you have them at a great time for you to promote the next team or company event. Whether it's a month away, a week away, two days away, six months away, three months away, whatever it might be.

If you've ever attended one of your company events you will know that you start to feel differently about the business. It is almost like instead of being on the ground floor trying to see the whole city, someone takes you up to the penthouse on the

87th floor where you take another look around and everything becomes so much clearer.

The feeling you get creates clarity and understanding for you to want to take more action. To go all in, make some sacrifices and stop playing the game small, in order for you to make a significant difference in your life.

Every year I hold my Success Summit event. This event is completely generic and is a place to come learn new skills, validate existing ones, hear from those crushing it inside of the Network Marketing profession, expand your vision and be around the right environment.

However, if the event conflicts with any company or team event, make sure you prioritise those events over any Success Summit event.

The third stage is you need to give them responsibility to make it harder to give up.

Kind of like the difference between when you don't have kids, versus when you do. If you don't feel like it one day, you just work through it. If you feel like quitting on being a Mum, you push through. You do whatever it takes because you are responsible for another person.

Same in Network Marketing. When you have a new customer or a new distributor, you will do whatever it takes because you don't want to quit on them.

Does it mean that you'll have 100% retention for everyone who becomes a customer or distributor? No. But it just means the rate will be improved.

By helping your new distributor or customer get a small win within their first 48 hours you dramatically improve the chances of that person lasting long enough to get a breakthrough in their mindset, transformation or understanding of what it is they have to do.

Not only does it add money to their bank account, but increases responsibility levels.

The simplest way to make this happen is to help them get a new customer. Whether it's their mother or father who buys the products, they have a close relative who decides to buy, or maybe it's their best friend who makes an order. Getting the win gives the feeling of progression which creates a good feeling, which leads to believing they can do it.

I remember my first small win was $18 in commissions by getting a few customers. To this day it is still the most powerful commission I have ever made in my entire life because it gave me the belief in the system and I knew I just had to keep going to increase the size of the commissions I would receive.

I Double Dare You to record the feeling you get the next time a good commission comes in.

The final stage is you need to make them feel appreciated.

Why? People who feel appreciated tend to do more, but also people don't like to leave an environment of appreciation.

Perhaps their partners aren't appreciating them, their bosses aren't appreciating them, their colleagues aren't appreciating them. Now, you might be someone who says, "Well, I get appreciation in my life." That's absolutely awesome, fantastic, but not everyone does, so you need to recognise their initial activity.

You need to post in your group, or shout out on your weekly Zoom call, "Congratulations to Mary. Mary has not only connected deeply to her why, she's also just booked tickets to the next event and is working on her first ever customer."

When people in your team see these posts or announcements they are conditioned to react in the comments, "Whoa, well done Mary", "Massive congrats Mary", "Go Mary, that's amazing."

Mary, although she has not made any money yet, feels appreciated. She's bought her products, she's joined the business and she's bought her event ticket.

When you combine the Infinity Cycle Of Success, Bridge Of Belief and the four stages of increasing retention, you'll be ready to begin the process of building your Network Marketing business for the long term.

PART TWO

I DOUBLE DARE YOU TO BUILD IT

CHAPTER 6
THE ROBBO RULE

During events, many people ask me, "Frazer, why do you open your mouth every time you smile?"

Look out for it if you ever see me at an event taking photos or on social media.

As I was growing up my parents decided to send me to a private, all boys school. It was interesting, everyone was trying to be the alpha male. Unfortunately, I had a really, really gummy smile, my teeth were all pointing in all different directions. As a result whenever I opened my mouth, the kids would make fun that I had a gummy smile and really bad teeth.

I actually didn't open my mouth so much as a kid.

If I did, I would put my hand in front of my mouth. Because of this I was quite depressed, very, very insecure, and extremely shy. My parents will tell you today that if the phone rang, I would run into the other room because I had a phobia of answering the phone.

It was really crazy. However there was one time of the week I really looked forward to. I loved sprinting. So every week we would have PE (physical education), and our teacher was Mr. Robinson, who we all called Robbo.

He was just the best. One of the first mentors I ever had.

I remember him coming to me at the beginning of one of the classes and asking, "Frazer, why don't you open your mouth? Why don't you smile? Why do you always put your hand in front of your mouth?"

I said, "Well, Sir. All the kids make fun of me."

He rolled his eyes and said, "Well, what do you love doing?"

"I love running" I replied.

He looked at me seriously, wanting to help, and asked "Okay, well, when you run and you run fast, do you smile?"

I said, "Yes I do."

"Why?" he said with an obvious tone.

I thought about it briefly and replied, "Because no one can see I'm smiling. I'm the fastest here."

He laughed, and started to walk away. A few steps later he turned around and shouted back, "Do you want to be really good at running?"

I shouted back, "of course!"

He pointed to the starting line and said, "Don't tell me, show me!"

What Robbo was about to say next would go on to revolution-ise my Network Marketing business, and I was 14 years old!

"The average 14 year old runs the 100m in 16.2 seconds. Are you going to be above average or below average?"

I laughed to myself and said, "I'm going to be above average, Sir."

He rolled his eyes again, this time at my new found confidence and replied, "Okay, great. Show me."

He would always get me to show him what I was capable of before he would coach me, I believe that is a trait of a great leader. Mentoring activity and not just words.

With his guidance I became one of the fastest sprinters in the school and was asked to join the rugby team to play on the wing.

For a while the strategy was pass to Frazer. I then ran, got tack-led a lot, but would score my fair share of tries.

The other problem I had as a kid was that I grew really tall, really fast, but I didn't fill out and I was pretty much built like a crisp. If you touched me, I bruised or broke something. Defi-nitely not ideal when playing rugby.

I was eventually asked to drop out of the rugby team because the risk of injury was so great, and this meant that I wouldn't be spending as much time with Robbo.

But the legend that he was, said he would still coach and

train me with my running and his door was always open for me.

Anyway, sometime later Robbo took the rugby team over to Australia to play a few games against some of the Aussie teams.

Whilst there, between two of the games, the team went white water rafting with Robbo. The raft capsized, everyone was thrown into the water. The lads were all panicking as they scrambled back into the raft. My friend then started to shout, "Robbo! Robbo! Someone help!"

Robbo was trapped under the raft. They couldn't get him out, and unfortunately he didn't return from the tour to Australia.

I remember getting the news. I was devastated. Absolutely devastated.

The one person who had helped me get over my fears was now not there for me.

Fortunately, my parents had gotten me into personal development throughout my school experience so I was able to continue my growth, get good dentistry and face my fears knowing that Robbo would have been proud.

By the way, if you have kids and are reading this right now, I encourage incentivising your kids to read some personal development books and have them complete a short series of questions so you know they have read it, then give them £5 or something similar.

When I eventually joined the Network Marketing profession, I found it incredible frustrating when anyone would join my team and then either did absolutely nothing, or even worse, just quit or went missing.

People would join the team and give me the Network Marketing kiss of death:

"Frazer, I am going to absolutely smash this. I will be the number one recruiter, I am really good at sales."

How many people did they end up recruiting? Zero, because they didn't even recruit themselves.

A few months had passed in the beginning of my career, I was recruiting people using the system in my first book 'I Dare You', but it got to the point where I knew I wasn't doing a good job as a mentor and therefore had to up my game.

I was sat at my desk and directly in front of me was a medal I won in a 100m race at my school in 2002.

I began to think, what would Robbo have done in the situation I am in now?

It came to me right away. Bingo!

Whenever I was given words by the people in my organisation I would say, "don't tell me, show me!"

I then went on to map out my "Triple A System".

1. Give an **Assignment**
2. Hold them **Accountable**
3. **Acknowledge** them in front of others

This would help me to identify the people I needed to work with, just like what Robbo did to me all those years ago.

Let's put it into an example for your Network Marketing business.

Someone joins your team. Congrats!

You now need to give them an assignment. This is where the Robbo rule really starts to come in, it works a treat.

"Your first assignment is to write your list. Most people aim for around 200, but just write down as many as you can, don't leave anyone off. Now, the average person completes this assignment in under 24 hours. Are you above average or below average?"

Did you see the Robbo rule work there? You are asking your new distributor if they are going to be above or below average.

Guess what everyone says? "I'm above average, Frazer."

What do you say? "Okay, great. Show me. 24 hours from now is going to be Wednesday 10am. So we'll have another call and chat then."

You have now set the assignment.

This is much more effective than adding people into a group and leaving them, giving them a 129 page getting started manual, or telling them they have to write their list or they are out!

Next step is to hold them accountable.

You will find out quickly, that there are three types of people.

1. The first type of person doesn't make the call at the scheduled time. They either vanish, give you an excuse, or look to postpone the meeting. They failed the assignment.
2. The second type of person makes the call at 10am on Wednesday. Good work. They passed. They got a C or a 6 out of 10.
3. The third type of person is the one who contacts you after a few hours of getting the assignment saying, "Frazer, Frazer, Frazer! I've done it! I've done it! I've done it!" If they contact you before the deadline then they have shown you with their actions that they want the next steps. They can't wait for you. They are hungry. They want to get on with it. Those are the people who you run with.

The final step is to acknowledge them in front of others.

Now is the time to celebrate the completion of the assignment by making a post in your group, sending something in your chat and/or mentioning it on your weekly meetups.

"Massive shout out to Mary. She has just written her first 200 list in three hours."

Your new distributor hasn't recruited anyone yet, they just have their list written, but think about how happy they feel being appreciated and respected by their peers. Perhaps for the first time in their lives they have won at something.

When their partners see this sense of achievement, even when they know they haven't made something yet they don't want to stop them feeling good about themselves.

Now you have stepped up!

The entire process of duplication starts by eliminating the overwhelm, giving clear step by step instructions and ensuring your new distributor knows the support is there.

If you don't have the upline to do this with, then be the upline to others you always wanted.

The Robbo rule is there to help you all identify the right people for you to run with, and start the process of duplication.

In the next chapter, we move onto the next assignment in the process to start turning that excitement into new customers and distributors for your team.

Oh, by the way, I smile with my mouth wide open now so all my teeth and gums are showing as I am making up for lost time.

CHAPTER 7
EXCLUSIVE ZOOM EVENT

I always think back to the day my Dad gave me one of the most important lessons I believe you can give someone in Network Marketing:

Understanding that once the majority of people learn something, they want to learn everything. It's a big challenge in the profession because people get stuck in learning mode and they fail to get started.

Your role in the duplication process is to get your new distributor winning as soon as possible. Remember in the beginning of this book where I shared the story of how I got started? That was due to my Dad getting me into action, fast.

When I asked him how do I invite, he told me to do what I would do if I was just inviting my friends round to watch the football game.

If he had given me an in-depth training on how to invite, I would have wanted to know how to handle objections, how to present, do I give teas and coffees at the meeting, how many should I get to the meeting, what do I need to do to close, how do I do it when I have no idea what I am doing, and all the rest that follows.

Instead you learn by doing, then you improve by teaching.

You pour fuel on the fire by then getting trained, reading books and attending events.

But those first few days are absolutely fundamental.

If you are following this book and studying it by making notes, you would have found that the first step is to actually recruit someone. Then it's time for the introductory call where the real reason for building the business is established. You can also share the details about upcoming events and give the first assignment to write their list.

Once they have done this and been acknowledged, the next step is for them to take part in their first "Exclusive Zoom" or E-Z (easy) for short.

All you need for this is a platform like Zoom, Skype or similar.

An E-Z is simply an online presentation that is ran by the upline and the guests are people who have been invited by your new distributor.

Now, obviously if your team member lives in Liverpool and their new prospect is in Liverpool, then great, they could do the exclusive zoom whilst at a coffee shop or in their home, and you could be on Zoom giving the presentation.

But to scale up, grow into different cities, build internationally and get smarter with the use of your time you are going to need to leverage the technology that is available.

An E-Z is the process of helping the newest team member gain a new customer in the first few days of joining, preferably within 48 hours.

HERE'S HOW IT WORKS.

Your team member is emotionally connected to their 'why'. They have a list of people and they're excited to take the next steps. You have built them up to feel good about their business and future.

It's vital to encourage them to take action with the list.

Here's a script to use:

"Hey Bob, all you need to do now is to invite five of the people you are most connected with on your list to an Exclusive Zoom that we will do tonight at 8pm. Don't worry, I will take care of the presentation for now. Does that sound fair?"

There are three types of people:

1. The first type will make excuses that they can't make it. Look to reschedule until they agree but understand that every day that passes reduces your chances of getting that quick first win.
2. The second type will ask what they need to say to get people onto the E-Z. Have them invite how they would naturally do it if they were to invite their friend to the cinema, to the pub, or for a meal round at their house. If they are really hesitant then give them one of

the scripts you have for your team, this is plan B.

3. The third type is the one who feels so confident and is so hungry that they just go invite people based on sheer enthusiasm and energy.

Before ending the call, it's time to set the right expectations to ensure you create a win-win situation for everyone.

Here's how you do that:

"Right, I am looking forward to your first E-Z. Here is the link to give to your prospects (enter Zoom link here) but I must tell you, the average person gets zero people attend their first E-Z. Don't worry if that's the case, you are just getting started and I will mentor you to get better".

By now, they have been given the next assignment, you've managed their expectations whilst not overwhelming them with countless trainings.

The majority of people want to learn before they do and end up learning so much they never do.

Now to the fun part of the E-Z. It's 8pm, the time has arrived,. There are only two ways this can go:

1. You and your team member is on the Zoom and no one else joins the E-Z.
2. You, your team member and one to five of their prospects join the E-Z.

It's important to note that most people will fail at their first presentation. Why? Because they scare themselves out of it. You don't want to give them a reason to want to quit because they've just spent a ton of time and a load of mone. Instead, why not do it at home so if they fail or when they fail, they haven't really wasted any more of their time.

In the first scenario, none of Bob's prospects joined the call.

This is now the perfect opportunity to mentor and train him based on the actions he has taken. He can share the messages or conversations he had to invite his friends onto the E-Z.

As long as your team member shows that they are taking action, you can continue to mentor them. The moment they stop taking action and just want to get on calls with you to talk about the weather or the latest episode of their favourite TV series is the moment the calls end.

In order to be mentored you first need to take action. You cannot mentor someone who is not willing to do the work.

The first E-Z call is there to again make sure you are working with the right people. Those who have the hunger and desire to succeed.

I dare you to step up your activity. The right mentors will notice your activity and amazing things will happen to you and your business.

In the second scenario, you and Bob are joined by two of Bob's friends, Mary and Sue.

The first thing to do is simply ask, "Bob, how do you know these two ladies?"

Bob can then naturally just share, which is a great way to start the call. It won't be perfect at the beginning but here is what I want you to really get about Network Marketing!

You can promise progress, but you can't promise profits.

After the introductions, simply interview Bob on his reasons for wanting the products and why he wanted to share with others to get involved with him.

You can then share what the products do for people, your story, some stories of others and the different options to get started.

Following that could be some questions and answers. It's essential to keep things informal, like a conversation between friends.

If you lack the experience to do the above, simply get to know Mary and Sue, interview Bob, then share a link to a video explaining what's involved. Whether it's in a group or independent website.

It might take you a bit of practice, but if you really want to level up, you are going to have to continue to step up. Time to show yourself and the world you're progressing!

Duplication is not just about what your team does, but what you are prepared to do too.

To finish the E-Z just make sure you give the next steps, whether that is asking "do you see this as a fit for you?" or you can set a time that Bob will follow up to see if you want to take the next steps or not.

Here's the most important thing:

Whether they decide to do it or not, it doesn't matter. Bob is learning the entire way. He's learned that he can invite. He's learned that you're going to be there and that he can leverage your time and experience.

You now have the chance to make Bob feel like a rockstar by acknowledging him again in front of others.

This is the key to crazy success in Network Marketing. Recognition.

Personally, you tell Bob after the call is done, "Bob, I just want to let you know the average person gets no one turn up to their first E-Z. You've just had two. You've got exactly what it takes to make this happen."

He's going to be excited. Even though the results haven't come in yet, he's thinking, I can do this. Then you tell everyone else in the group or messenger chat that Bob has just had two people attend his first E-Z.

Inspire the team by showcasing action taken by your team, not just the results. Your company will highlight the results.

You will notice that the right people in the team will want to impress others by taking more action.

Not everyone will get results, but everyone can take action if they make the decision and commit to it.

Again, you have followed the Robbo rule.

You gave the assignment to invite five people to the E-Z.

You held them accountable by giving a time the E-Z will be starting.

Then you acknowledged them personally for taking action if none of their guests attend and you acknowledged them publicly to the rest of your team if they got people attend the E-Z.

Now, I advise having a 3 strike rule.

This is simply in place to ensure people aim to improve and you continue to work with the action takers.

If none of Bob's prospects were to turn up to three E-Z calls in a row, then you need to ensure Bob can introduce his prospects to a cloned version of you or another leader and tune into the group training instead of continuing to do calls with no one.

Your time is precious. You would have done 3 mentoring calls by this time too which is plenty for people to know how to invite in the right way at the beginning of their journey.

You don't have to have the 3 strike rule but remember you can't push a piece of string.

You can tell Bob, "We have got the Facebook group. All the tools and information are in there as well as versions of the presentations. Feel free to use that. We will also have the weekly trainings and you have my number. I am here whenever you need."

I will be covering this more in one of the upcoming chapters.

However, if he keeps bringing new people to the E-Z, simply mix things up to ensure his development as an upcoming leader.

If he gets new people onto three, four, five E-Z in a row, you're now going to ask him to step up.

"Bob, you have massively impressed me over the last week or so. Are you ready to hit the next level?"

The answer is always yes, you have the right person.

"I want you to learn the process to what we are doing here because next time I want you to lead and I will come in to share my story."

Record the calls so you can give them a copy to review.

The more people on your team who are capable of running presentations and calls, the better your team will be. If it is just you then you have a business that is dependent on you being there.

Sometimes you have to throw your team in the deep end. That's how I learned. That's how my Dad learned. That's how a lot of people learn. If you want to spring it on your team member on the day that you are going to have them run the E-Z then go for it. I just feel that a little preparation can go a long way.

Imagine if you were teaching your new distributors to learn the presentation when they first started, they would be completely overwhelmed and would be paralyzed with fear.

That's the Exclusive Zoom process. It's very, very simple, but you have to help people launch their business.

By this time, they've not made a single social media post. They've only spoken to five to fifteen of their closest friends if they have done 3 E-Z.

You've told them they'll probably fail, however they still have a list of people and are emotionally connected. This process works if you work at it. If you're thinking this is too long winded and laborious. You've got to understand that Network Marketing takes work and human connection. It's fundamental.

The next chapter reveals how to use social media in the right way to create curiosity and not give the game away.

CHAPTER 8
YOUR SOCIAL MEDIA LAUNCH

I always get really excited for people when they join the Network Marketing profession. The potential they have just unlocked in their lives becomes a reality at the starting line of their journey of growth and development.

Most people who join also get fired up, and they should, it's exciting, but there's a saying in Network Marketing that's been around for a long time.

"Ignorance on fire beats knowledge on ice."

This can be true when it comes to inviting people. People hear the energy in your voice, the way you act, something is different, and they want to see what has gotten you all pumped up. However, it isn't so effective when it comes to posting on social media. Here's why:

You can't read tonality.

When people put up a post that says, "Oh my gosh, I'm so excited. I have joined (enter company X) and now looking for people who want to earn an extra income."

They get no likes or comments and start to blame the algorithm for their failure.

It just doesn't work. How do I know?

I did it.

A few months ago I was on social media and a memory came up of a post I made 10 years ago. I had written what I shared above.

I cringed. It was so embarrassing. Why did I even do that?

But it was an amazing reminder that people still do this when they are excited to tell their social media friends and following what they have got their hands on.

So how do you launch on social media? What should you post to get things going?

Well, if you can't read tonality, how can you get your energy and enthusiasm across in a way that helps others to catch on fire? Whether you are confident, shy, experienced, clueless, extroverted or introverted?

Live video.

Whether it's a live video of yourself sharing what you will be doing, a video post inside of the stories on your social media platform or a live video interview with the person who you joined the company with.

Yes you are going to feel uncomfortable. That's normal, but I will show you a way to feel comfortable and get the best results possible.

Your goal is to grab someone's attention and then provide enough value that they are interested enough to keep listening to the conversation that you are creating.

Think of it like walking down the street and seeing a £20 note on the ground. It grabs your attention and you know its value.

A few moments later you pass a penny, it grabs your attention, but you keep walking passed as you feel it is not worth it.

You need to be able to do something that is not normal for your friends and followers. Then provide value in a way that they want to be a part of the conversation and get involved without knowing all the details.

In fact, my Dad always tells me, "Frazer, the key is to tell them everything, but nothing".

Get them excited by the idea and concept, but not what the ingredients or details are.

This is where most people fail on social media, especially when launching. They wonder why all their friends and followers aren't interested. They make a post which no one likes, they feel that it's because the algorithm limited the visibility.

But your friends saw it. So when you go to contact them they think "Oh, Bob's going to try and get me into this thing he posted about the other day."

They're already resistant before they even know what it is. You've lost the curiosity.

I believe the best way is to utilise live video interviews to launch your business onto social media.

HERE'S HOW IT WORKS.

Step one. Get together with the new team member and arrange the date and time for you to do the live video to launch their business onto social media.

Step two. Set things up so you have something to promote. You are going to have to get good at promoting if you want to go far in this profession. Whether it's a video, system, event, story, mentor or book, it doesn't matter. The best promotors make the most money.

I recommend using BeLive.tv – it's a website that enables you to go live onto Facebook at a scheduled time, allowing you to promote a link to your friends and followers. As soon as the broadcast begins, the screen will be split. This allows both of you to be live from the beginning.

If you have trouble with BeLive.tv another option is to use Zoom.us and you'd be able to stream your Zoom onto your Facebook page. It's basically allowing you to do a live with two or more people on at the same time.

Step three. Discuss the questions that you will be going to ask your new team member. This way your social media following see you being interviewed and think, "Whoa! What's my friend Sally done to be interviewed? That's really cool."

Remember, as the mentor, always do things to test the team member to see if they are willing to do whatever it takes to succeed. This helps identify the next potential leader on your team.

The lazy team members probably won't do it.

Step four. Share a script for your new partner to start to contact their friends and followers to tune into the live at the scheduled time. This one works well:

"Hey Mary, I've got something really exciting happening at 8pm tonight. Can I count on you to help me out with it?" Or, "Hey Mary, hope you're well. Are you free at 8pm tonight?"

Maybe they reply with, "yes, I am."

You would send, "Cool, well I'm announcing something really exciting at 8pm with one of my friends. Can I count on you to be on the call to support me?"

You're inviting your friends to attend the live. Because you have the scheduled live, you can grab the link, and send it to them. You could also set reminders inside the messenger to remind you to send them the link.

Now this is a little bit different to you inviting them to an E-Z because they're just going to be watching the live. But it's a way to expose something and then follow up after.

Step five. Do the live. Start at the arranged time and go through the questions. It should take about 10-15 minutes. At the end of the live, have a call to action where you say something like:

"So guys, I will actually reach out to you personally to get your questions answered. If you want to skip ahead, as you see what we see, just send me a private message and I'll get back to you."

This is absolutely fundamental as there will be some people

watching who you didn't invite, who maybe don't know you, who don't engage on things posted on social media, but they want to know more information. Now they know what to do.

Step six. Have your new team member follow up with all the people they invited or people who engaged in the live. For the people they invited, reach out and say, "Hey Mary, so what did you like best about that live? You excited?"

If anyone shared, commented or liked it, reach out to them and say, "Hey, thanks so much for supporting my live. Just curious, would you be open to some more information about what it is? No worries if not, I just thought I would ask".

The other way of executing on this process, is for you to create a group and then add people into the group and do the launch live in there. Obviously it takes a little bit more setting up. You have to create a group, give it a name, create the cover photo, write the description and get people to join it. Then of course you will only be getting those inside the group actually seeing the live. No organic reach.

I would just stick to your profile because you're going to reach more people.

When it comes to the questions, just ask your new team member things like:

- "How did we get to know each other?"
- "What pain do you have in your life?"
- "What are you looking to get out of this project?"
- "Why do you want to use these products?"

The goal is to relate to the right people who are watching or to get someone who is watching to share it with someone they know who is dealing with issues discussed.

The final part of the social media launch strategy is to ensure you continue to use the stories feature to document your journey of transformation.

People will be able to follow your journey after you have launched. You can even mention that you will do this, on your live interview, so people continue to follow the progress.

The first one could be a selfie video of you saying, "I'm starting my journey today. I'm super excited. I am about to jump on the scales to weigh myself for the first time!"

Day two might be, "Today I am so pumped. I have much more energy, I had such a great night's sleep last night."

These are just two examples. But the whole idea is that instead of a before and after photo, people get inspired by your progression. You also might not have the time to wait for the perfect before and after photo.

In years to come this content will be super valuable to you. In fact, my biggest regret in my Network Marketing career, was that I didn't document the beginning of my journey.

I wish I had the footage of me crying the first time I spoke on stage. As well as the photos at small meetings, with 5-10 people.

This process helps new team members launch on social media. It also allows them to keep putting the business and products in the faces of the people watching, without sharing what it is, and therefore messing it all up.

Don't feel like you must follow this process to get success. But if you want to test the team, push them out of their comfort zone. As well as continuing to show that you are there to help, it can be fun.

CHAPTER 9
DUPLICATABLE SYSTEMS

It's my belief that mentorship is the key to creating a long lasting residual income from the Network Marketing profession. You will be able to establish and develop leadership within your organisation, which in turn will lead to having a business that is not dependent on you.

However, you will need a system to serve the masses so that your business can still operate whilst you are doing other things. Like living your life, or working on developing the leaders you have identified.

I shared the story, towards the beginning of this book, of the time I was served by a young man at McDonalds who looked like he had just woken up.

Ever since that day I have been fascinated by systems and processes to make things more simple and effective.

In fact, the word SYSTEM itself is an acronym for "Saving Yourself Stress Time Energy and Money".

Some of the companies I loved to observe, which rely heavily on using systems, are Starbucks coffee shops, Subway sandwich stores, McDonald's restaurants and Ikea furniture stores. Every store runs the same way, is laid out the same, and even the uniforms the staff wear are all the same.

The flatpack furniture that Ikea sells always makes me laugh.

You order the flat pack. It arrives at your home, or you pick it up from the store. You then unbox it and lay all the pieces out on the floor along with the basic tools. Lastly, the little white manual.

There are three types of people: those who pay attention to the little white menu; those who ignore it completely; and those who get someone to put the furniture together for them.

But here's the thing. The system is so precise that every single person who follows the instructions inside of the manual, pending they have all the screws and tools, complete the process. The completion rate is exceptional.

Ikea have created leverage and independency. They create the flat pack pieces and the manual, then they sell it to you. You now have to construct and erect the furniture independently. They have now taken the time to perfect their system, they leverage a little manual with a step by step process, and they let their customers build the product.

It saves them time, money, energy, and that's what system stands for.

You're going to need four different systems in order for you to create an environment where everyone can win. They are:

1. Lead generation system
2. Product exposure system
3. Business exposure system
4. Team building system

The first system, for lead generation, is to ensure no one runs out of people to talk to on the team. I highly recommend my "FAM" process.

FAM stands for Find, Add, Message.

You find someone on social media, add them (or follow), then message so they know why you would like to connect. Usually the intention is for the connection. Remember, conversations come before commissions.

Now the best way of doing this, is for you to just block out five to fifteen minutes a day; usually in the stolen moments. Like when you're picking up your kids. Perhaps you're waiting for the toast to burn? Obviously my favourite is good, effective use of toilet time.

I dare you to go on a winning streak. Just find, add and message someone new every single day. Whether it's just by adding one, two, three people. Remember your minimums will create your maximums.

What you do daily is what will actually build the business long term. Not what you can do in one day.

I get asked every day, "Frazer, how many people should we be adding per day?"

There isn't an optimum number, it doesn't exist. Everyone is different. The FAM system is in place to make it simple for you to never run out of people to talk to.

This will help to avoid overwhelming people who just want to work the business in their spare time, but also allow those who are working all the time to do more if they feel they need to.

I always say in order to grow you've got to find your flow.

So just work on what your sweet spot is in terms of adding new people, ensuring that you message them once added. You can follow what I share in 'I Dare You' for the best strategy on that.

If you win the day, you have a shot at winning the week.

If you win the week, you have a chance to win the month.

If you win the month, you have a great chance of winning the year.

If you win the year, you have an incredible opportunity to have massive success in Network Marketing.

By doing the FAM process with your team you'll be pouring the fuel on the fire. Meet up once, twice, three times a week, for 15 minutes. Host the call and instruct the team to find, add and message others.

Have people count the number of FAM's they do in the 15 minutes to set a team record as well as their own personal record.

You need to teach the team that the absolute minimum they

should be doing on a daily basis, is to grow their list. As long as you grow your list, you have a chance of succeeding in Network Marketing.

The second system is to have a product exposure system.

First thing you need, is the platform. Some teams and companies use a website where you can send people to in order for them to get the relevant information. Others use Facebook groups that allow you to add people into the group to get the information. There are also many people who use a daily, weekly or monthly call, webinar or Zoom where they present the information.

For product exposure, I personally prefer and recommend using a Facebook Group as the platform, especially if you are wanting to build on social media.

In 2012 I came up with a system called FITEF, yet another acronym:

F Find someone.
I Invite them to join the group.
T Tag them in the comments of the relevant information / video.
E run a live video as an Event each week.
F Follow up with the people who you invited.

It was simple and easy to follow. However, a few years later I heard about the ATM strategy. Yet another acronym, so I paid full attention!

A Add someone into the group.

T Tag them in the comments of the relevant information/ video.

M Message everyone you added after they had reviewed it.

Although they are both the same concept and idea, ATM is easy for people to remember and therefore execute on. Just make sure people are inviting people to join a group by asking if they would like to be added, instead of just adding someone in.

You will also need the tools. I recommend either using the company tools that might already be available, or recording a presentation from one of the best presenters in the company who is available to you. I personally prefer cloning the presentation from a leader and leveraging that one.

The great thing with a system is that it will help you to NOT change the message, but simply change the audience.

Remember, don't be a fool, use a tool.

By leveraging a video that was carefully created once, you can put hundreds of people onto the same video knowing it will do the right job. Then all you have to do is add people into the group, tag them in the comments of the relevant tool and message them to see what they liked best!

The last thing is you need the other members of the group to share their product stories and testimonials.

Groups thrive off energy, especially when there are a bunch of posts every day that are relevant to what the group is all about.

You should also have someone inside of the team (can be crossline if you decide to have one huge group for the entire organisation), to go live every day either demoing the products, sharing their story or giving value around the product.

People want to know what the product does. Share how it can help, the problem it solves, and how it has worked for you and others. In my opinion, having one group for all, is better. If you try and create hundreds of groups for everyone on your team you are diluting the energy.

The third system is to have a business exposure system.

This is a completely separate group for people who want information about the business. You can create the culture inside of your team to ask those who they invite to the product group, as well as the customers they have, if they would like to be added to the business exposure group.

The script you could use is, "Hey Mary, just curious to see if you are interested in finding out how you can make some extra money leveraging our awesome products? No worries if not, just thought I would ask."

Although the business exposure is very similar to the product exposure group in the way that there are tools and testimonials, obviously about the business instead of the product. There needs to be some sort of live event each week too and eventually, every single day.

There's just something different, the energy and the engagement level of a live event is much, much higher than that of a recorded tool.

It is also something your team can invite to and follow up once finished.

This can be done as a live business presentation into the group, or even better, done as a webinar or Zoom call away from the social media platform.

You will need the business presentation tool and others sharing their business based stories as well as some product testimonials. It's also good to have daily lives inside the group based around what the business can do, incentives, and even basic recognition to inspire others to join the next call.

TOP TIP: With both the product and business exposure system, make sure you utilise the group cover photo to give 3 steps to take. For example:

"Welcome to (Group name), to get started, follow the 3 simple steps:

1.   Watch the video at the top of the group
2.   Introduce yourself to the rest of the group
3.   Engage in the posts that interest you"

For the business one you could even add a link and date to the next live event. Obviously, you would then need to change the graphic each time.

The fourth and final system is to have a team building system, also known as an onboarding process.

This is the process put in place so that when someone buys the product or joins the business, they have some simple steps to get things set up and moving. In this chapter I will be covering the business side of the onboarding process.

- How do they arrange their welcome call with the upline?
- How do they get to do their first Exclusive Zoom?
- How do they get to know how to do a social media launch?
- How do they get to know about lead generation, the product exposure and the business exposure systems?

You would have a group for your team members only, no guests.

This is where you create your own version of the Ikea flatpack white manual, the simple steps to follow in order for them to get set up and feel good about their progress.

So, let's go through this to give you an action plan.

Someone new joins your team group. Let's call her Mary.

Step 1 is for you to have a welcome call with her. On this call you help them emotionally connect to the business, give their first assignment of writing their list, schedule the next call or chat to hold them accountable and tell them about the next event.

Step 2. At the end of the starter call you tell Mary that you are adding her into the team Facebook group and will tag her into the welcome video. You can also give her a basic template or instructions to introduce herself to the group.

I prefer having people introduce themselves as it creates independency from the get go, instead of you doing it for them and creating a new partner who is dependent on you.

Step 3 is to have the follow up call to see if Mary completed writing her list, then give the next assignment to invite five of her contacts to her first Exclusive Zoom call with you.

Step 4 is to recognise Mary for taking action, inside of the Facebook group.

Step 5 is to help Mary do her social media launch following the process shared in the previous chapter.

Step 6 is to set up weekly accountability calls with Mary to mentor her through the stages of growth required.

That's it. Keep it simple. Now, throughout these steps you can tag Mary in some videos or files inside of the Facebook group so that you are completely effective with your time.

If you are having to do things that can be taught via a recorded video, then you are wasting time and not creating independence or leverage.

Utilise the units and files section inside of Facebook groups to put checklists and tutorials. Just know that if people can see hundreds of different steps and trainings right away, it can create overwhelm and therefore prevent them from taking action.

It was Albert Einstein who said that there is genius in making complex things simple. Simplicity is the key. Once this is all set up, you're done. Once you've created the system for someone to buy the flat pack (the business) and the manual (onboarding process), all you have to do is FAM people, expose them to the business, and give them the next steps.

It's important to note. If you are part of a team that already has these sort of systems in place, leverage it. There is power and energy in numbers and collaborating as an overall group.

Remember, you are always on the lookout to identify the next success story. That person is the one who is going to be taking the right action.

You need to work with the action takers and forget the action fakers.

As I shared in an earlier chapter, not everyone is going to succeed. Most people aren't even there to build a business. They just joined because they want to be a part of a community. Some people have just joined because they want to meet people. Maybe they have seen photos of the events and just want to attend those.

Creating these systems allows you to establish positive boundaries quickly and ensure people get excited about the business, fast, and not overwhelmed then quit.

If you can get people to generate leads and understand the culture and the community, that lead generation is the aim of the game. Without a lead, you can't get customer. Then you show them how to expose the product, the information about the product. Then show them how to upgrade a product user into a business builder. Then how to actually onboard and get that business builder starting to generate leads, get people into the product, and then obviously get business builders. You are going to win.

CHAPTER 10
3 WAY MESSENGER CHATS

I remember when I was struggling in my Network Marketing business. I wasn't following a fundamental step that my Dad kept telling me to do, and that was three-way calls.

I see a lot of people struggling with their Network Marketing business because they don't utilize the power of three-way calls. I think one of the reasons is because a lot of people are now afraid to get on a call or it's just not as normal as it used to be. In fact, if I get a call, it gets declined.

Most people aren't calling each other these days. They are using messenger apps like Facebook, Instagram, WhatsApp and iMessage to communicate.

In 2013, I had a defining moment in my Network Marketing business.

I travelled to the east of Russia, for the first time to do some meetings with my team, in a city called Ulan-Ude. When I arrived there I realised very quickly that I hadn't packed the right clothes to cope with the conditions of minus twenty five degrees celcius. I also came to notice that no one spoke English.

It was a great trip. We had some great meetings, the translators were amazing and people were joining. However, when I left to go to an event in Moscow, I wasn't able to do the presentations or calls with them because no one was available to translate.

During the flight to Moscow, I decided that I would do 3 way chats with my team and I would use Google Translate to understand what the prospects were saying, then type something back to them in Russian.

They were blown away!

"Frazer, speaks Russian", they all started telling everyone.

I didn't have a clue how to read, write or speak Russian however I was leveraging a technology that was available to you and me, for free.

Side note. At that event in Moscow, I met Svetlana. She was the daughter of a friend from one of the members on team. She interpreted me, and the rest is history.

Anyway, I came back to the UK and decided I would start doing 3 way chats with my English speaking team.

It was fast, simple, didn't require any time to schedule appointments just to be let down by others, and I didn't have to be skilled or teach people to be skilled on the phone.

It also allowed my team to ask questions inside of another chat when the 3 way chat was going on as they could reply to their prospect whenever they wanted.

Finally, it served as a training because my team members could go back through the chat to see how I ran things, and pretty much copy and paste.

Using the strategy of 3 way chats, instead of 3 way calls, allowed me to build an organisation that was filled with over 80% of people who were non-English speaking as well as them living in a time zone different to the one I was in.

HERE'S HOW IT WORKS.

Once someone has reviewed the information inside of the product or business exposure system, you would follow up with them by saying, "Bob, what did you like best?"

Make sure your exposure systems are there to weed out the serious from the curious so that you are using your time most effectively on the 3 way chats.

When the interest is there you would then create a 3 way chat. This includes you, your upline (or collaborator) and your prospect.

The first and most important part of any 3 way chat (or call), is proper edification. The definition of edification is the process of improving the perception of someone.

Once you have your group chat set up, you should do a short voice message to introduce both people to one another. This should last no more than 30 seconds each. If you want, you can also create a written edification so you can copy and paste it. Just remember people can't read tonality.

This creates credibility between your prospect and collaborator, it allows your collaborator to know how you know each other and helps them to understand what part of the process they are up to. It also gives you the chance to compliment your prospect.

An example of proper edification inside of the 3 way chat would be:

"Hey Sue, I would love for you to meet my friend Mary. Mary is an absolute rock star and is actually the person I work with daily and if you decided to join this business, you will also have the chance to work with her too. She is completely financially free from this business and she's going to be able to help you every single step of the way."

Then the next message:

"Hey Mary, I want to introduce you to my friend Sue. We recently connected on social media. She has seen the business information and I thought we could chat some more. She is a go-getter and someone I believe would be awesome at what we do, a future rock star for sure. Can you share your story and vision with her please?"

Now Mary, your collaborator – meaning someone you decide to work with who might not necessarily be your direct upline, or within your upline at all, could be side-line or downline. She takes over and shares why she believes the opportunity is so great and helps answers any questions that come up.

You can now learn the sort of questions that get asked and will be armed with the answers.

The cool thing about 3 way chats is you are able to leverage someone's experience, skills and time to get your prospect over the line to join. They might also be the one who does the close.

This process of 3 way chats also works really well when some-one joins the business. Although having calls after someone joins is best. It might not be possible with time zones. If that's the case, set up a three-way chat and introduce your friend, your business builder, your new customer, to the upline so that they feel a hundred percent secure in the fact that they've got the support they need.

I hope you are excited. It's all starting to come together.

You have unlocked the ability to believe it and build it. Now it's time to boost it. Let's switch gears and establish how to boost the process, starting with three different strategies on how to get duplication by creating a large amount of activity in a short space of time using themed days, surveys and referral posts.

PART THREE

I DOUBLE DARE YOU TO BOOST IT

CHAPTER 11
CREATING GROUP MOMENTUM

At this stage you will be able to take action on a personal level and be in control of the activity you are taking. But in order to create momentum you need to ensure that many others on your team are doing the activity as well.

Personal momentum creates group momentum. When you have some groups hitting momentum, it turns into team momentum. When a few of the teams inside of the company hit momentum then that turns into company momentum, which eventually turns into industry momentum.

That's my goal.

To help you and your team get into momentum, to allow your company to get into momentum and the knock-on effect, the industry gets into momentum.

If you don't already know it, my mission is to raise the professionalism in Network Marketing done online, to unite the industry and to make it sexy again.

In order to create the necessary activity, you have to create an environment where anyone can win. Remember the story of the soil and seed?

Of course it's good to become a better seed, but the environment is more manageable, and in your control. However, you cannot control the quality of seeds that come into your organisation and you certainly can't control the activity they take.

So, how do we actually get the team planted in the right soils to create group momentum? Well, it needs to be simple enough that they know exactly what to do on a daily basis.

Therefore, I use a concept that I like to call "themed days".

Each day from Monday to Friday has a different theme. Saturday and Sunday is not necessarily themed, but there are different things the team can be doing throughout.

- Monday is usually "Messenger Monday".
- Tuesday is known as "Transformation Tuesday".
- Wednesday is "Survey Wednesday".
- Thursday is "Testimonial Thursday".
- Friday is "Follow-Up Friday".

Let's break each day down so you know how to implement them right away.

Messenger Monday involves you and the team reaching out to new people to see if they are open to checking out some information about the product or business.

If you are using the lead generation system, which is all

around the FAM process there will be no problem with your team ever running out of people to talk to.

On Monday morning, make a post on your Facebook group or however you communicate with the overall team. The post can read something like this:

"Today is Messenger Monday! Reach out to at least one person today, using one of the scripts in the files section. Once you're done, let us know by leaving a comment below!"

You can also put the scripts in the comments section.

The reach out could be something like, "Hey, Bob. Just curious, would you be open to checking out some more information on an exciting project I'm working on? No worries if not, just thought I would ask."

Another reach out could be, "Hey, Bob. Real quick one, do you know what residual income is?"

Another one could be, "Hey, Mary. Hope you are good. Really weird question. Are you happy?"

When you combine a large number of people who all do a small amount of activity, you will begin to create the momentum you desire.

Transformational Tuesday is where you're going to be sharing a business based transformation story of someone inside of the company who has gone from zero to hero, or from Loser to Legend.

You can create some ideas for posts inside of the files section of your Facebook group and encourage people to post their transformation post in the group when they reach that point. That way you have a library of stories your team can repost.

It can be a photo of the person, or one of you and them, with a longer written story above. You could do a Facebook Live and talk about it. Maybe you print off a photo of that person before they joined and now after attending the company incentive trip. Lastly you could share it in a series of three or four different story posts.

Now imagine if you have hundreds of people in your team eventually all doing that. You will get people's attention, especially when they see so many transformations. They are going to want to find out more.

The companies and teams that have won the most on social media over the years are the ones that are all seen doing the same things. People are exposing the transformations so that others simply need to know what it is because they feel like they're being left behind.

Again, like what you do on Monday, create a post to remind people of the day, where to find stories to use, and to comment when done.

Survey Wednesday is my absolute favourite and here is how it works:

On Wednesday, obviously, you're going to reach out to people who you're already connected with and send a message like this:

"Hey Mary. Would you be open to answering a really quick one question survey for me? It would massively help me out."

Guess what? The majority of people who see that message and reply say, "Yes."

You now want to ask a simple multiple choice question that is linked to your product.

For example.

Let's say you have a coffee product, you would say, "Great, thank you. Do you prefer Starbucks or Costa Coffee?" That's it.

If you have a travel service, ask "Do you book your holidays on booking.com or hotels.com?"

If you're in the health and wellness space, message "Have you ever used a health supplement? Yes or no."

If you have a skincare product, say "Do you prefer Nivea or Dove moisturiser?"

Go and research what the most popular products are in that space in your market, so that you're going to reach the most number of people who can answer it very easily.

This is where many people mess it up.

Let's say Mary replies, "I prefer Starbucks".

Most network marketers will respond by sending, "Well, I've got this amazing product that you need to try out, here's the link to check it out."

No. Simply say, "Thank you so much. I really appreciate it," and then use what I call my Data, Paper, Later strategy, also known as DPL.

DPL is where you collect the data from the answer to the survey, put it on paper, for you to use later. Simple.

You're going to then leverage the answer that was given to you on Friday by simply saying, "Hey Mary. Just wanted to say thanks again for helping me out on that survey the other day. Quick one, would you be open to checking out some information on a game-changing skincare product that I've been using, which has really helped me out and many others? No worries if not, just thought I would ask."

The whole goal is for you to get data, put it on paper, and then you leverage it later by asking a question relating to the survey you asked.

Think about what will happen when there are thousands of surveys being done every Wednesday and then thousands of people being followed up on a Friday. What do you think is going to happen to the energy within the team?

Again, make a post in your Facebook group to remind everyone of the theme. You can brainstorm and share ideas of survey questions to ask inside of your groups too in order to mix things up.

Testimonial Thursday is very similar to Transformational Tuesday. Instead of sharing a business based transformation, you're going to share a product story.

Whatever type of post you did on the Tuesday that week, do something a bit different. So if on Tuesday you did a Facebook Live, then on Thursday do a series of stories. If you did a long post with an image on the Tuesday, do a Facebook Live on the Thursday. Mix it up.

Remember the posts should be sharing what the product does, and not what it is. People want the solution to their problem and how to take the next steps, not a list of ingredients.

Imagine if a large number of people in the team are doing that. The exposure is massive.

Just keep remembering to make the posts in the morning to remind the team of the theme, how to find examples, and to comment once they have done theirs.

Lastly, Follow-Up Friday is imperative. The majority of Network Marketers know that the fortune is in the follow-up. However teaching this can be difficult as they don't know when is best, or simply cannot track the people they're speaking to.

My recommendation is to teach the team to note all the people they have asked to see if they are open to checking out some information, whether that was on the Monday or Wednesday, or when they are talking to people on social media outside of their "theme time".

Some like pieces of paper and a pen; some like using spreadsheets and some prefer CRM systems. It doesn't really matter what system you use. It matters more that you actually do the follow-up.

When Friday becomes the day you follow-up with people you will actually keep in touch more as you can put their name in the diary to follow-up again and again and again, in one, four or eight Friday's time.

The follow-up message you send depends on what you are following up on, but it could be something like this:

"Hey Bob, so sorry I've been so crazy with all that's going on at the moment, that I forgot to follow up with you. Were you interested in checking out more information? No worries if not."

Or it could be something more simple:

"Hey Bob, just wanted to follow-up with you. You good?"

Now again, imagine when Friday is absolutely banging in your team because everyone is following up which then leads to more exposures, 3 way chats, and sales into your business.

I know I keep repeating myself, but make sure you make a post inside of the group to remind people of what the theme is, where they can find some ideas of what to send in their follow-up, and to post once they are done.

If you want to increase the chances of people actually commenting on the post once they have completed, do a prize draw each week by choosing one of the comments from some of the posts.

Those are the five different theme days. Throughout the week they're not just doing that. That's just a thing that they can do literally within 15 minutes a day. It's a basic daily activity, so they're not necessarily doing the exact same things, but everyone in the team is doing the exact same things.

My favourite part about it all, is you end up creating a collaborative space because everyone can then help each other out to say what messages they are sending, what surveys are working best, what posts are getting results, and what is getting response when following-up.

You can add it all into the files section of a Facebook group to make it simple for anyone to know what to do.

You can then train the team to tweak what they are currently doing instead of training new things that they are not ready for.

I love the example of Formula 1. The car goes out for a few laps of the racecourse. It then comes into the pit stop. Does the team change the entire car, the driver and the engine? No. Instead, they tweak the wing on the front of the car. They tweak the little valves. They maybe change the tyres. They tweak the engine settings. They make tweaks dependent on the conditions and what's going on.

You shouldn't need to change things, it can create confusion. You just need to tweak parts of the process that people are working on.

There are also two other different processes for you to be able to create group momentum that I want to share with you.

There needs to be a simple process for you to be able to upgrade a customer into a distributor.

The majority of the organisation will be more comfortable talking to people about the products because they either got results themselves from the products and so joined the business to share with others. Or they feel more comfortable selling a product, than a business opportunity.

This process all starts from the moment you get a new customer who has just bought some product from you.

You get a customer, congratulations.

After 24 hours you should follow-up to confirm their great decision, the product is on the way, and expected to arrive soon. If you can give the date that's a few days after the date you know it will arrive, then great, under promise and over deliver.

This will help eliminate something that is very common, called buyer's remorse.

When the product has arrived, make contact regarding the usage of products and show them how to get comfortable with it. Then encourage your new customer to post inside the product exposure group to share their excitement.

Keep the communication open with your customer. After a certain milestone, depending on the products, contact them and ask this very simple question:

"Hey Mary, I noticed that you've been using the product for 90 days now. Can I ask a really quick question?"

"Yes, sure." Mary will reply.

"On a scale of 1 to 10, how open would you be to sharing your product experience with other people?"

Now, if Mary was to say one, two, three, four, five, you would just say, "Hey, that's absolutely awesome. Thanks so much for letting me know. I appreciate it."

If Mary was to say six, seven, eight, nine, or ten, you would then excitedly say:

"That's really cool. Just curious, would you be open to checking out a way how you could monetize your product experience or potentially get your products paid for by the company?"

It's a way where you introduce your customers to the business opportunity, depending on if they feel comfortable sharing their story.

Make note, just because they might say one, two, three, four, five to sharing their product story, it doesn't mean that they don't want to reorder. So use that simple process for you to be able to get business building conversations with your customers.

The last process I want to share is exciting and involves asking your customers to refer other people to you without giving you their friends names and numbers.

Referral posts are where your customers can get customers without actually joining the business or you could get customers from your already existing customers without them already being business builders.

HERE'S HOW IT WORKS.

You want to carefully create and craft a referral post for your customer to actually post on their own newsfeed or story. It could be something like this:

"Ahh I'm so excited. Thank you so much Bob Jones for introducing me to this wonderful product. Without it, I would be

7 kilos heavier. I have tried so many different things but this is the one! If any of you would like Bob to hit you up with the product that I've been using, feel free to drop a fire emoji down below or reach out to Bob personally."

You can create your own version, but that's the idea.

Tell people you are excited, tag the person in the post who introduced you, give a short compliant testimonial (check with your company first), then give the steps to get more information.

Now as the person who got this customer to make the post, you can go and contact the people who potentially comment on the post, and get the information to them.

Every company is different, but if you're able to have customers who can enrol other customers, then you would put them underneath your current customer. If not, you can agree to something that brings benefit to both you and them.

I am a great believer in that the more customers and users of the products you have, the more chance you have of upgrading the right people into your team who have a deep connection with the products due to their potential emotional transformation.

CHAPTER 12

TRACKING YOUR NUMBERS

When building my Network Marketing business, fortunately a few of the leaders owned traditional businesses. I remember going to visit one of them, when he was about to close his restaurant for the day. As I arrived, he was filling out this really weird piece of paper.

I asked him, "What are you doing?"

He replied, "Oh, I'm doing my numbers. At the end of every day, I track my numbers. Things like the amount of product I've sold, the amount of money I've spent and I do all the numbers so that I know where my profit was."

I was shocked, I thought an accountant would take care of all that.

He said, "I need to be able to predict what's going to happen tomorrow. How will I be able to do that if I don't know what happened today and the previous days? I need to use the data."

The lights were going off in my head. I had a huge bingo moment.

What if I could predict someone's future? That would be gold.

After returning home and figuring out a few different things. It was simple:

If you know your numbers, you will be able to predict your future.

Before I share how it works I just want to explain something extremely important that helps you understand the true power of this.

In order to truly succeed in Network Marketing you need to understand that activity multiplied by skills equals results. Increase your activity, as well as your skills, and your results will improve.

However, too many people focus on having results-based goals and not activity-based goals and get disappointed the moment they don't reach their desired result within their first month.

Ever heard someone say, "I want to make $10,000 a month within my first year", then they miss their "goal" and go quiet?

It happens all the time.

I hope that you are starting to realise after reading this book that you have to create the culture within your team of taking activity that eventually get the results you want. But let's focus on the things we can control, and track them.

HERE'S HOW IT WORKS.

There are only five activities you need to track, every day.

1. The number of people you connected with using the FAM method

Once you have found, added and messaged someone, put a number one using a tally chart. When you do another, make it two and so on. Don't wait for someone to accept your friend request or follow you back before sending the message. You can control the process when you find, add and message people.

If you feel overwhelmed with all the people and lose track, here is what I recommend doing.

When using Instagram, flag the conversation inside of the messenger, then at the end of each day or week, add up all the flags.

When using Facebook, screenshot the chat so it saves to your photos app. Then at the end of the day or week, add up all the screenshots of chats you've had.

2. The number of people you ask to see if they are open to the product, service or opportunity

Whether you do this right after connecting, or building some rapport and relationship first, is your decision. However, you need to ask your new or existing contact if they would be open to seeing some information.

This will be less than the number of people you are FAM'ing so most likely easier to track daily using your tally chart.

3. The number of people who review the "tool".

Whether it's a video in a group, on a website, you host a live online presentation, maybe you run a home or hotel meeting, perhaps you meet up with someone in a coffee shop, track the number of people who have seen the tool.

4. The number of people who say "YES" or "NO" after reviewing some information

If someone says to you after watching a presentation, "Yeah, I'm in," then they join and become a customer or distributor, put a one on your tally chart. If another person who see's the tool says, "No, I'm not interested," put a two. Don't separate the yes's from the no's, you just combine them to give your total.

5. How much commission you made that week or month (depending on how your company pays out).

This is pretty straight forward. You get paid, it's in your back office or bank account and you make note of it.

However you want to track is up to you. What's important is that you treat your business like a business and know what activity you took that day.

By the end of the month you will be able to add them all together to give your monthly activity report.

Your monthly report, once you add all the data up to give the monthly total could look something like this:

1. Number of people you FAM   300
2. Number of people who asked if they were open   60
3. Number of people who reviewed the tool   30
4. Number of yes or no's   10
5. Commissions $600

Here's where it gets exciting.

Using some basic math, you can determine what you get paid per activity you took.

So if you earned $600 for getting 30 people to review the tool, whether they said yes or no, you earn $20 per person who reviews the information about the product, service or business!

The formula is:

$$\frac{\text{Monthly commissions earned}}{\text{\# of people reviewed the tool}} = \begin{array}{l}\text{Commission earned per} \\ \text{person who reviewed the tool}\end{array}$$

You can even do this based on asking people if they are open, regardless of their response.

Now you are able to predict your own future, but more importantly, the future of your team members.

This is what you're going to do.

On the first of the month you have a call with those you are working with to review their monthly report.

You ask, "How much do you want to earn next month?"

Your team member replies, "Oh well, I made $600 last month. It would be great if I could make $1,200 this month."

Notice that your results have doubled. What do you think needs to happen to the activity for you to get the double results?

Simple, you need to double the activity.

All you would do is next to the numbers on the monthly report, write the new month's number.

"Right, well you had 30 people review the tool last month. You will need to have 60 people this month, which is 2 a day."

The more data you gather, the more accurate your numbers will be.

It is of course a rough idea. It might take a few months for the math to work out correctly but it is a great way to inspire your team into taking action.

You can also use this to set accountability milestones. So if the goal is to get 60 people to review the tool, that is about 20 people every 10 days. Making sure your team is on track is how you step up as the mentor, ensuring the correct activity is being taken and not just training all the time.

On the topic of training, what do you train on?

Well, armed with someone's monthly activity report, you are able to see where people are going wrong, especially when you know your team's average "commission earned per person who reviewed the tool".

When people's goals are set on activity and not results, everything changes.

Why?

Because the majority of people who set goals, don't hit them.

It can be off putting when you keep setting goals and fail to reach them. However, following what I have shared, every single person in the organisation can win by completing their activity goals.

With time, the commissions earned per person who reviews a tool will grow. If I was to look back at the commissions I earned, then divided it by the number of people who watched a presentation, a video, or attended an event, it would be over $1,000 per person. Would that be worth it?

When you know the power behind Network Marketing, you will start to see the importance of getting as many people onto the presentation as possible.

Bill Britt, a Network Marketing legend, said it best, "show the plan, show the plan, show the plan", (in our example, the plan being the tool).

Now, you and your team are going to deal with a lot of rejection and being told "NO" a lot. It's part of the process.

As the number of people you ask grows, the number of no's you get grows. You have to create a situation where you celebrate the no's.

I remember the day I created this concept. One of my leaders came up to me at a convention we were at in 2012. He pulled me to one side, and told me that one of his leaders had quit. My immediate reaction was that I was upset for him.

However, his reaction surprised me.

He started to laugh and did the dance that I used to do whenever I reached a new rank. We both started to do it. Others from the team came running over asking what was going on.

We turned to them, whilst laughing and dancing, and told them that one of his leaders had left.

They all started laughing and dancing too.

What is now called the "Ninja Dance", was born.

I fully recommend you create a team dance, something that's easy to do, so that whenever someone gets a no, they have to take a video doing the dance, and post it into the Facebook group along with the reason why they are doing the dance, for all to see.

You don't dance without a smile on your face, so when others see Mary dancing because someone called it a pyramid scheme, said it's a scam or that its's too expensive, people laugh it off and realise they are not the only one getting no's.

The love the videos get from the team also motivate people to keep going. Sometimes people just need to be reminded that they are doing the right thing by building a business and promoting the products that have done so much for them per-sonally.

As the team grows, it does get a little bit crazy. You can just dedicate one time slot per day where the admin opens the group up for videos to be posted. Perhaps you do them on your weekly Zoom call.

It's just a great way to lighten up the mood around negativity. Because when you truly know you make money from the no's, everything changes.

I Dare You to start tracking things and have your team do the same thing. They can read this book to understand why they should do it. Inside my Inner Circle group coaching program, I use this process every single week with the members. If you would like more information on that, just send an email to info@frazerbrookes.com with "INNER CIRCLE" in the subject line and I can get some information over to you.

CHAPTER 13
EVENTS TO SKYROCKET YOUR BUSINESS

Looking back at some of the defining moments of my career, inside of the Network Marketing profession, I am reminded of how much I learned from my parents.

My Mum taught me almost everything about being a good human being. Be someone who listens first, speaks second, always treat everyone like a someone, as well as so many other wonderful things.

My Dad mentored me by giving me business skills and always ensured I was in a positive environment whenever I was not in school.

One of the moments I remember very clearly. It was one evening when it was going dark. My Dad came into the kitchen my Mum, brother and I were about to eat. He looked at us and said he was going out to a meeting.

I looked at him shocked and said, "at this time? It's going dark!"

I was only about six at the time.

He sat down next to me and said, "Frazer, one day you will come to understand, that in the Network Marketing game, more meetings means more money!"

My Dad was right. The more meetings or events you do the more money you can expect to make.

It's no coincidence that those in the profession attending and promoting more events, are earning more than those who are not attending and promoting events.

When I joined the profession myself, I made the decision that I would run all sorts of events, not just business opportunity events that everyone seemed to be so fired up about.

Again, I sat down at my desk, and created my four-part event strategy, called ABCD.

These events are very simple to do, highly effective, and if you do all four of them, you can expect your business to skyrocket.

A stands for **Accountability**.
B stands for **Business**.
C stands for **Culture**.
D stands for **Duplication**.

Let's break each one of these down one by one, so you know how you do them, what's involved and why they are important.

I touched on the accountability event briefly in the previous chapter. You should be having some sort of event with your personal team members and those you have identified as upcoming leaders, at least once a week. Of course you would be doing the monthly activity report call on top of this.

I recommend doing the call towards the end of the week, usually on Friday.

Ask them what their activity has been for the week, what their win of the week is, as well as what they have struggled with. Just having this weekly check-in ensures they stay plugged in to the business.

It also allows you to improve your mentoring skills, as well as learn when someone is most likely about to quit when they don't turn up to the calls each week.

Another idea for an accountability event is to post in your Facebook group every Friday asking what their wins of the week has been.

The post could look something like this:

"Hey guys, it's Friday! No matter how big or small, what's been your win of the week?"

People absolutely love to share what their win of the week is.

You can then start to look through the comments and in the following week give a shout out to some of them.

"Congratulations to Terry. Last week he was able to (enter Terry's win of the week)".

If you are able to give prizes for those that you highlight then that will encourage people inside your team to share their wins. It can motivate people when they see so many wins, they start to understand they are in the right place, and need to take advantage of it.

It's all about creating an environment that people do not want to leave. Remember, it's the soil, not the seeds.

The business event is simply a business exposure.

Whether it's an in-person event, a Zoom, or even a Facebook Live in an exposure group, this should be done at least once a week.

However, when your team is in momentum, having them once a day, even multiple times a day is highly advised, especially if you have an international audience. If your team is English, Russian, Polish, or Spanish etc. speaking, you might have to have different presentations on different days at different times for time zone and language differences.

There needs to be an event that people can invite others to, because people promote a live event much more than they promote a recorded video.

The next type of event is the most important for long term growth, increased retention and a whole heap of other reasons. They are culture events.

Culture is the key to duplication, retention, long term growth, residual income and to create a thriving life inside of Network Marketing.

This is broken down into two parts.

1. The training you provide
2. The events you run

Yes, there are other things that create the culture, but these are relating to the events.

The culture of the team should not be training for the sake of training. It should be discovering what's needed in order to overcome their challenges.

You do this by creating a secure, yet vulnerable environment.

This enables you to help your team understand that it's ok to have a breakdown, because that will be followed by the break-through.

If you do this correctly, you will find that people don't leave. The environment is too important to them to be around.

People pay therapists hundreds of dollars an hour just for someone to be able to hear their story in a safe and secure environment. They are too afraid to tell their partners and friends about the issues they have in their life.

However, you have the opportunity to help people.

HERE IS HOW YOU DO IT.

Step 1. Have the calls on a Wednesday or Thursday

Step 2. Introduce the call and give some updates, maybe some shout-outs to people you know are making things happen.

Step 3. Ask everyone to let you know what's been their win of week so far in the comments. You can unmute a few of the people's microphones so they can share quickly too.

Step 4. Now you are going to ask people to raise their hand using the feature on Zoom if they want to share their struggle.

The first few times you do this, you might have to share the struggles of the week you're having. This goes against the grain of the Network Marketing saying "don't be negative to your downline". However, I think in the world we live in, authenticity is our opportunity to become a leader people want to follow.

Step 5. Unmute someone who raises their hand and have them share what it is.

Step 6. Instead of answering it yourself, ask the rest of the people on the call to comment or wave on the camera if they have ever dealt with anything like the struggle that was just shared.

Guess what? Five, ten, one hundred people show that they have dealt with the same struggle. Sally, who's been struggling with inviting her best friend to check out the business, now knows that it's not just her and she's not the odd one out. She's not alone. She feels that she's already found her people.

Step 7. Ask the people on the call who has overcome the same struggle Sally is facing. It could go something like this:

"Thanks for sharing your struggle Sally. You can see loads of people are sharing the same struggle as you. Has anyone had the same struggle and been able to overcome it?"

Step 8. Unmute the microphone of someone who has said they have been able to overcome the struggle Sally has been facing, and have them share how they did it.

Here's the great thing about this:

Not only have you filled Sally with the belief that she can do it. You have armed her with what she needs to do in order to have a breakthrough. But you have also now removed yourself from the equation and created independency.

Bob is now training Sally on how he was able to overcome the struggles she was facing.

Whether Bob is in Sally's organization or not, you've created a collaborative, secure, vulnerable environment where people are prepared to have a breakdown by sharing their struggles, in order to have their breakthrough.

The second part is to do with the events you run with the intention of growing the culture.

As often as you can, at least once a quarter, arrange to meet up just to hang out and brain storm. The three things I believe you must do to create a solid bond that creates the necessary culture is:

1. Laugh together
2. Cry together
3. Hug one another

You can do the first two on Zoom calls. But the third one requires you actually getting in front of people.

When your team is smaller and lives locally, meet up to go bowling. As it grows, have a big barbecue.

Have Leaders Days where you have people round to your house when they reach a certain rank in your company.

When you continue to expand, arrange to meet up the Friday night before your team training, or have a team lunch at your company convention.

Create a leadership retreat where you spend 2-3 days together somewhere fun.

The whole idea is for you to spend as much time with your team as possible. Not because you have to, but because you want to.

We live in a world full of lonely people, and by creating a culture of togetherness, it gives people the chance to step into their full potential to impact others who were in a similar situation to them.

When you create the campfire that people want to be around for long periods of time, people catch fire themselves. Armed with what I have shared so far in this book you are going to turn them into a wildfire.

You don't become big news by being a campfire, you have to become a wildfire.

By focusing on the events to build culture, you will have created the campfire to get there.

The last event is the duplication event. This is the easiest one for me to tell you about because it's the company convention or conference.

You will get true duplication when you have people go to a big team or company event.

Now, if your company has events every quarter, plug into them. If they have two a year, plug into them. If they have one a year, plug into them and create your own team thing if you're able to, six months after.

There's no coincidence that the person who has the most people at a company event is the one who earns the most.

Take the time to tell yoru new team member about the next event on your starter call as well as creating a campaign for the team to heavily promote the next big event.

Set a team goal, let everyone know what it is and create a plan of action to make it happen.

As a great believer in the power of events, I created Success Summit for anyone involved in Network Marketing. Here you will have the chance to come and see the bigger picture of the profession. As well as learn skills from other leaders who share what is working for them.

You can learn more by visiting www.SuccessSummit.info

These are the four events to run. The accountability every week or month, business exposure events at least once a week, culture events on Zoom every week and get togethers every quarter if you're able to do that, then the duplication event with the company convention.

Combine all those four and you will have the soil rich enough for any seed to grow.

CHAPTER 14
BLITZ'S AND CHALLENGES

We have reached the final piece of the puzzle, the last part of the masterpiece, the final step in the process for you to create the magic in your existing and future organisation.

I remember being in a city called Udine, not too far from Venice in the North Easterly part of Italy. The leader of that team within my organisation had arranged a few meetings and had me come over to be the guest speaker.

For me it was a bit surreal. I was 24 years old being invited to speak around the world on how Network Marketing had changed my life.

Anyway, we did a few meetings. They went great, and at the end before we all left we decided that the day after the event, I would be available for anyone to bring their friends and contacts to. I would simply stay in the lobby of the hotel I was staying at in the middle of the city.

We did a blitz session where by all the people at the event would invite a few of their friends to join them with me the next day.

I woke up on that Monday, went down to have breakfast at the hotel. I don't remember exactly what I had, but it was most likely yoghurt, granola and some fruit. I finished eating, got out of my chair, left the breakfast room and started walking to the elevator, hit the button, the doors opened, and just as I was about to step in, someone shouted, "Frazer! Frazer!"

As I turned around, one of the members from my team was stood with two of his friends.

Unfortunately, I hadn't had a shower at this point. However, I did a small meeting, simply sharing my story and the steps they would need to take to earn the income they had suggested to me they wanted to earn in the conversation.

One of the two said yes, and joined on the spot, the other one said she would think about it and was never to be seen again. Not in a murderous way, I just didn't hear from her again.

As that meeting ended a few more people had come to the lobby. The same thing happened. I shared my story and gave the next steps.

This process kept repeating. It was now 1pm, I had done about 8 meetings and I still hadn't had a shower.

By the end of the day, we had signed up 25 new distributors into the team, all from one to three prospects at a time.

I finally was able to shower and then sleep!

Crazy thing happened though.

A few years later I went to Kazakhstan to build my team. We

used a similar process of people inviting their friends after a small event, to then meet with me in the lobby of one of the hotels in Astana, the capitol.

The morning event had six of the leaders, who then invited people throughout the day.

By the end of the day, we had spoken to over 400+ people. They were all then invited, whether they had joined or not, to come back that evening where we would do a more formal meeting in one of the event spaces at the venue.

Close to 500 people showed up. It all started with a few people doing a blitz session.

The reason why I share this story is that in order to create momentum you are going to need to take a lot of the right action in a short space of time. The magic happens even faster though when you have a group of people taking the right action in a short space of time.

I am not telling you to go and do presentations in hotel lobby's in Italy, whilst smelling like you live on the street, work a little smarter.

Therefore, the online blitz formula was created.

Here's how it works.

You would have your team join you on a Zoom call. If it's just you for now, then just do this process on your own or collaborate with an upline or side-line.

The call would last 15 to 30 minutes and you would focus on

one or two activities that you all do together. Some activities you could do include:

1. Find, Add, Message
2. Commenting on other people's posts
3. Reaching out to people to see if they are open
4. Following Up
5. Event promotion

Step One. Start the call at the agreed time.

Step Two. Host and introduce the call, give some updates, shoutout those taking action, and remind them all about the next event or training call on Wednesday / Thursday.

Step Three. Tell everyone what the activity you are going to be doing will be.

Step Four. Set the timer on your phone, or find a countdown timer on YouTube. I recommend setting them to 10 minutes.

Step Five. Have them keep track of their activity within the 10 minutes so you can have them share their score at the end. Go!

Step Six. Once the timer hits zero, have everyone stop and count up their total score.

Step Seven. Have the participants share in the comments what their total score was and be sure to shout them out.

Step Eight. Unmute some of the team to share how they were able to get such a high score (remember, all based on activity).

Step Nine. Ask if anyone struggled and see how, as a group,

you can help them breakthrough the challenges they are facing.

Step Ten (optional). Repeat the process with another activity.

That's it. It's not rocket science. I recommend doing at least one blitz call a week, usually on a Monday to create some momentum. You could even call it Momentum Monday.

Once people know how to do the assignment they can do it with or without you. But when they know they can get on as a group and show off their skills by getting a high score, or by helping someone who is struggling, they are more likely to take action.

Eventually you can use this format and do calls every day, maybe in different languages and time zones. Just be sure that other people on your team will help out so it's not dependent on you, remember!

Earlier I touched on the themed days. Why not do an online blitz call around each day? Having a blitz on a Friday just to follow up with people you spoke to that week can be very powerful.

Now let's talk about one of my absolute favourite things to do with your team, challenges.

As a leader in Network Marketing your job is to make the boring, exciting.

Challenges make this possible. They can last five, ten or fifteen days, you decide.

The purpose of challenges is for you to be able to have opportunities to involve everyone in the organisation, the chance for you to be able to shout out anyone in the group and make them feel special, not depending on their results, but activity taken. You also want to be able to send them something that they treasure forever.

You will find that running challenges create the necessary environment needed to thrive.

These challenges are done away from the main team group. You will need to create a new group that is open for the duration of the challenge, then is removed. This allows you to get the team members who want to take part to commit to it.

To ensure it works, focus your energy and attention on that group during the challenge. They are committing to being action takers!

The five day challenge is perfect when your company might announce an incentive, new promo, discount on a product, or maybe launch something completely new. It's also awesome to run a five day challenge to help promote a big event.

The ten day and fifteen day challenge is where you're going to be doing a Facebook live challenge to build confidence in your team to go live. It could be an Instagram story challenge to get more people exposing their personality, mission, products or business. Perhaps you run a pipeline building challenge where you just have people following the FAM process.

Think of it as a series of blitz calls, that last a certain length of time, where you document the activity taken to be able to establish if someone finished what they started or not.

At the end of the day, it's a challenge. You're supposed to be pushed. But by doing this, not only will the activity on your team increase, but also their skillset and mindset.

The key to the challenge is having daily accountability.

I highly recommend setting up a Google form where the participants complete at the end of each day. Have a deadline so it needs to be done otherwise you will be eliminated.

When people are given the assignment and then held accountable they will take action.

You will be able to download all the data that is submitted on the form. This will allow you to gather it all together and create a leader board to recognise those who took the most action.

Anyone can reach the top of the leader board as it is based on taking action, and not getting results. Of course, the more action you take, the more chance you have of getting the results. But the overall team needs to see that they have the chance of becoming a champion.

Now if you ask for your teams mailing address on the Google form you will be able to acknowledge the action takers. This will ensure you complete the Robbo rule of assignment, accountability and acknowledgement.

Have a simple A4 certificate created to say that someone has completed the challenge. Write their name on it, and send it to their mailing address. You might need someone to help you with this as your challenges grow.

You will notice that your team freak out over receiving the certificate.

They feel accomplished, they feel special. They feel unstoppable.

Perhaps they share it on social media, which creates curiousity for more people to reach out to ask, "Hey, what's the certificate for?"

People will do more for praises than they will ever do for raises.

Network Marketing is one of the best industries in the world to get recognition. Don't just recognise those bringing in the results. Make the masses feel special, let them taste what the big recognition must be like, by celebrating the fact they took part in the challenge and are a valued member of the organisation.

CHAPTER 15
I DOUBLE DARE YOU TO DO IT

You might be reading this thinking you have a lot of work to do. But if you seriously want a thriving Network Marketing business that continues to grow month to month, year to year, then it's going to take work.

It's going to take some time to set things up. It's going to take time for you to integrate this with your existing team. The new people coming in, this is all they will know.

Just remember, the goal is to make the boring stuff exciting by creating the best environment.

Now you've learned how to become a better leader, more powerful mentor, realise belief levels need to be high in order to dominate, the strategies to actually build the business and that you can only boost something once it's built.

You now know that the soil is often more important than the seeds.

The seeds will thrive in the right soil and die in the wrong one, or give up before the time comes for them to flourish.

I want you to lose the laziness in you. When you recruit someone you haven't closed a sale and be done. You have opened up the chance to completely change someone's life. But it is going to take some work from you, and them, to get them up and running.

If you get someone started in the right way, by following what I have shared in this book, you have the chance at creating a legacy that your family will be proud of. Do you want that? Are you be prepared to do the work?

I Double Dare You to believe in it.

I Double Dare You to set assignments.

I Double Dare You to hold people accountable.

I Double Dare You to acknowledge your team more than you've ever acknowledged them before.

I Double Dare You to step up as a mentor and run Exclusive Zooms.

I Double Dare You to get people to have a social media launch.

I Double Dare You to create duplicatable systems.

I Double Dare You to start doing three-way messenger chats.

I Double Dare You to use surveys.

I Double Dare You to have and use themed days.

I Double Dare You to use a customer upgrade system and use referral posts.

I Double Dare You to start tracking your numbers.

I Double Dare You to run accountability and business events.

I Double Dare You to create culture events using Zoom and hold offline events.

I Double Dare You to get more people to your company event than ever before.

I Double Dare You to utilize blitzes and challenges...

...and *I Double Dare You* to actually finish what you started.

You can do it.

Whether you believe you can or not, sometimes you just need someone to tell you. Whether it's a mentor, parent, friend or even me.

You have to sometimes be told, "You know what? I believe in you."

If you're someone who doesn't get that anywhere else, now that you've read I Dare You and I Double Dare You, I truly believe that you can do it. You just have to follow the principles, put your own spin on it and create a unique culture.

Obviously, leverage what I've created here, but go and be the voice that people need to listen to.

Go and be your true authentic self.

Go and create the environment that your team want to spend

time in, instead of running out of it like you would in a traditional job.

Go and create a place of security and appreciation that people never want to leave.

The goal of a Network Marketing professional is to bring people into the business. Identify the people who you need to work with and then create an environment that people do not want to leave from.

That's going to be how you get to a stage where your income is truly residual, but more importantly, your children or future family, tell you:

"You know what Mum? You know what Dad? You're my hero."

There is no greater success than that in the world.

I Double Dare You to go and make a difference.

FURTHER RESOURCES

I DARE YOU:

If you haven't already read the first book, the ultimate guide to building your Network Marketing business using social media, go to:
FrazerBrookes.com/book

I DARE YOU COMMUNITY:

For more content, updates, early access to upcoming Challenges and Bootcamps, as well as future books and a place to get your questions answered, join our dedicated group:
Facebook.com/groups/idareyoubook

SUCCESS SUMMIT:

Every year Frazer holds one of the biggest generic Network Marketing events in the world. Success Summit has been designed to raise the professionalism of the industry and to bring the best strategies that are working for top performers from many different companies and countries.

For more on this game changing event, go to
www.SuccessSummit.info

WORK WITH FRAZER:

If you would like to work closely with Frazer, check out his Inner Circle coaching program where you will have the chance to be mentored by him as well as the following:

- Weekly Accountability Check-Ins
- Online Mastermind Calls
- Personal Access To Him via WhatsApp
- Weekly Masterclasses To Grow Your Business

For more information on how you can apply, send an email to **info@frazerbrookes.com** with subject link "INNER CIRCLE".

SOCIAL MEDIA PLATFORMS:

- Facebook Profile: **Facebook.com/fbrookes**
- Instagram: **instagram.com/frazerbrookesonline**
- YouTube: **youtube.com/c/frazerbrookeschannel**
- Facebook Page: **Facebook.com/frazerbrookesonlin**e

WANT FRAZER TO TRAIN YOUR ORGANISATION?

Frazer can coach, train or speak for your organisation in a number of ways, but most common and popular are:

- Live Event – whether it's a company convention, team event, leadership retreat or other.
- Online Calls – whether on Zoom or via Facebook Live into a closed group.

Frazer specialises in:

- Social Media Recruiting
- Online Duplication Strategies
- Network Marketing Core Skills
- Belief Building

If you would like Frazer to train your organisation, send an email to **info@frazerbrookes.com**

My final double dare for you is to post a selfie holding the book. Let me know what you loved most about the book, use the hashtag #IDareYouBook for your chance to win prizes.